THE POVERTY ASSASSIN

"Responsibility has no shelf life."

MALCOLM ALLEN

The Poverty Assassin

Copyright © 2019 by **Malcolm Allen**

Web: www.Unconditional.org
ISBN: 9781072371816

FOREWORD

BY BENJAMIN CRUMP, ESQ

RESPONSIBILITY HAS NO SHELF LIFE

R esponsibility has no shelf life. I've seen that principle at work throughout my life. In my work as an attorney representing victims of crime, poverty, and racism, I've witnessed the tragedies that happen when individuals shirk their responsibilities.

Every morning 325 million Americans wake up to this world, with all its laws, requirements, and duties. Sadly, more than two million wake up in prison cells. Many of these inmates got there because they denied their responsibilities, but too many of them are there because someone else wouldn't step up, and do the right thing. We are responsible for our decisions, and whatever consequences they have. That's true of everyone everywhere.

One of the greatest allies of those who seek to evade responsibility is poverty, or as Malcolm Allen names it in this book: "The Poverty Assassin." According to the U.S. Census Bureau, poverty affects 12.3% of all Americans. That's nearly fifty million victims, many suffering from isolation, malnutrition, and lack of proper healthcare. Like any skilled killer, the Poverty Assassin isolates its victims so it can pick them off slowly, one-by-one. In our efforts to improve our communities, one day we concentrate on schools, the next day we turn our attention to housing, then maybe nutrition, then mass incarceration. Our proposals to solve these are sincere, but they almost always fall short. Why? Because we avoid the responsibility that goes with the apparent problem: poverty.

Poverty is everyone's concern, but it hits African-Americans hardest. While 9% of whites live below the poverty threshold, the figure for African-Americans is 28%. Children and young people are also more significant risks, with 22% of them falling victim to the Poverty Assassin. But while those who live in poverty can't evade their role in creating their condition, we who have the money are the most responsible. We are the ones with bank accounts, diplomas, and property. We have the jobs and own the businesses. In return for our affluence, we must take responsibility for the truly needy.

Recently we've seen violent cases where rights and responsibilities seem to clash. Often there are overtones of racism in these conflicts. Most of these cases involve life-and-death choices where one person's decisions affect families and whole communities for many years to come. That's always true when you make decisions about matters of life and death. You're responsible for those decisions, and all of their potential consequences. You can't "move on" from such an act. From that moment, until you die, your ongoing life will be affected by the decision you made. You might work toward positive ends, or do wrong, but none of us can escape our responsibilities. We can face them and find solutions, but, if we ignore them, we'll eventually discover that responsibilities don't have expiration dates. Once again: Responsibility has no shelf life.

That principle has been echoing through every state, city, and town in our nation. We can see the conflicts arising from it in Baltimore, St. Louis, New Orleans, Washington, and L.A.

Poverty is the responsibility of every citizen. As it victimizes fifty million Americans, the rest of us have to open our eyes. Each of us must do whatever he or she can to provide education, training, and employment for every citizen. We must equip our schools and teachers to deal with the effects of poverty in the classroom. School lunch programs could be broadened to include a good breakfast for every student. Well-nourished students will be better able to learn. After-school activities could be tailored to help students improve reading, writing, and math skills. Many school programs depend on parents and the participation of other citizens. We must volunteer our time, and find resources in our communities, to educate our children, improve our schools, and provide jobs for those who are graduating. If there are no jobs in our community, we must attract more businesses, or start businesses of our own so that we can hire our fellow citizens.

In the end, we are all responsible for each other. Americans of all races are discovering that in schools, churches, homes, on the street, and in the workplace. Responsibility knows no shelf life. It doesn't end after a week, or a month, or a year. It is the continuing duty we have to everyone around us, and it is their obligation to us as well.

The recent unrest in America's cities arises from lapses in official responsibility. Some law enforcement agencies have allowed their officers to ignore rules and regulations that guarantee rights, and often save lives. They've turned a blind eye to racism and encouraged rough tactics. They've developed an attitude of "might makes right," and twisted "zero tolerance" policies to serve their self-interests. They've done this in communities that have already fallen victim to the Poverty Assassin. The citizens of these communities are desperate. Each day they suffer from violence, but when they call the police, help is a long time coming, if it gets there at all.

Responsibility knows no shelf life. Though you might be limited in what you can do about the wrongs you see, that doesn't mean you can ignore them. Malcolm Allen is taking on the most profound injustice of all: the Poverty Assassin. Mr. Allen sees the problem, imagines solutions, and inspires us with stories and examples of those who have escaped this assassin's wrath. Mr. Allen dodged those bullets, leaping beyond the Poverty Assassin's reach, to build profitable businesses that help lift people out of the prison of poverty. Then they too can accept the responsibilities freedom brings.

Though many of us live in communities that seem to have little faith, we can create hope by accepting full responsibility. If we have a failing school, we must fix it. If we have brutal or ignorant law enforcement, we must demand better hiring standards and training. If our neighborhood lacks business enterprise, we must create it. We can defeat the Poverty Assassin, and undermine all the negative forces within our communities, only by accepting our responsibilities every day. Mr. Allen is answering the call and showing us how.

CONTENTS

INTRODUCTION

W hen we think of the word "assassin," most of us conjure up images of James Earl Ray, Lee Harvey Oswald, John Wilkes Booth, and all notorious killers of great leaders down through the ages. The assassin pulls the trigger, the great one falls dead, and the world changes for all of us. Some of these individual assassins are hired killers or agents of conspiracy. Others are frustrated losers who want to make history. They succeed. The killers of Dr. King, JFK, and Abraham Lincoln robbed us of visionaries who tried to make the world a better place. In each of them, we lost our hopes and dreams for a better future.

But what about the assassin who targets everyone? This isn't a disturbed individual. It's not even a human being. This is a subtle, inhuman, often unintentional conspiracy of mindsets, systems, and emotions that join together to kill our spirits. No one person hires this monster to do its dirty work. It has no mother or father. There's no evil genius directing its moves. It's formed by customs, traditions, and thousands of subtle details that converge into a way of life. This cruel assassin can drag us down if we let it. All we have to do is the easiest job of all: nothing.

This assassin kills as surely as any murderous thug with a gun does. It targets the poor, the sick, the young, the elderly, the uneducated, and many more. It's the most prolific assassin in history, laying waste to neighborhoods, cities, and even whole societies and nations. Living in the richest country in the world is no protection. A recent survey by the Associated Press showed that four out of five Americans live in the path of this assassin, and, at some point during their lives, they suffer the wounds it so easily inflicts. An American traveling abroad can witness entire regions and nations felled by its bullets of hardship and want.

This assassin has a name: Poverty. The only hope of stopping it is with us. Individually, and together, as a community, we must arrest this killer, removing it from our streets and homes. We can do this by taking action.

This book is for anyone who's willing to face this threat and ultimately banish it. Has the Poverty Assassin touched your life? Without even knowing you, I can confidently say: Yes. Eighty percent of Americans have experienced direct onslaughts from its varied arsenal. Every single one of us suffers from its indiscriminate attacks on our nation's homes and families. You might have been born into a family whose talents and best intentions were eaten away by this assassin for generations. Or maybe the Poverty Assassin caught you in the crosshairs of its gun sight in these last few years, as our economic boom went bust. You might be one of what's termed: "the working poor." That's those of us whose wages barely cover the necessities of sustenance living. But even if you have a good job, even if you own your own business, even if you are rich, and have never had the slightest worry about money, the Poverty Assassin plays a part in your life.

As anyone who's lived in both worlds knows, hard times touch us all. To avoid the assassin's wrath, the rich must shut their eyes, build walled-in, gated communities, or stay far from the centers of commerce where their riches are produced. Those who are only comfortable must drive along the edges of poverty, avoiding certain neighborhoods, while they close their eyes in a vain attempt to escape the sight of it. Yet, if they have the slightest sensitivity, they still can't help but feel its dark presence. Those who've just recently climbed up from of its pit of misery will always know it as a vivid memory.

I know the face of poverty from my own upbringing, and the work I do every day with people, institutions, schools, churches, and organizations worldwide. I grew up in the northern Louisiana town of Lake Providence. In 1997 it was the subject of a *Time* magazine article titled: "The Poorest City in America." In the downtrodden neighborhoods of Lake Providence, no one would've blamed my family if we'd thought of ourselves as lucky. Though we were surrounded by the Poverty Assassin's victims, we'd been spared. My father had a decent job, and there was always food on the table. Nonetheless, the assassin's influence permeated our household. In that tragic community, it couldn't help but infect us, right down to our very souls. All around us were people with little to nothing who seemed to have no choice but to feed off each other's misery. Crime, ignorance, prostitution, and disease were daily facts of life. Our schools were literally falling apart, with shortages of everything from pencils to qualified teachers. Healthcare was a joke, though no one was laughing. Depression wasn't a mental state; it was a reasonable reaction to the world we lived in. As a child, I had no idea that there was any other way of life. The Poverty Assassin defined my world.

The sadness of that permeating sense of impoverishment wormed its way into our home, sapping our family's spirit. Though we were doing better than most of the people we knew, there we lacked hope. Life was a vast emptiness to be endured to the end. The notion of happiness never even entered into our thinking. We knew of no way to take action, and besides, we were so beaten down we had no strong desire for change. That would've required a strong will, as well as a seemingly impossible optimism. Instead, life was what it was, and you just had to take it.

That's how it works in the closed-in world of a town or neighborhood that's fallen victim to the Poverty Assassin. The children grow up not knowing any better, and the grown-ups are too weary to care. That's what happens when the Assassin's bullet pierces the heart of a community. It bleeds out a little at a time, not quite dying, but hardly living either. It's as if an entire community goes on life support. It can't eat or breathe on its own, yet its feeble heart keeps beating. Visitors find a warm body that's just barely recognizable as human.

It doesn't have to be that way.

Circumstance, and some hidden spark of desire, combined to help me escape Lake Providence, and its harsh, self-destructive mindset. By the time I got out of my teens, I'd joined the Navy. It was the only escape route I saw. Finally, I traveled to other places. Once I had some perspective, I realized that I lived in a nation that was rich beyond my farthest imaginings.

In the Navy, I went to the Middle East and served my country in the first Gulf War. Later I was a part of the mission in Somalia. In those distant lands, I saw very different societies, but they shared the same desolation and want—gifts of the Poverty Assassin. The people had their own customs and traditions; their land, climate, and vegetation were totally unlike ours, as were their faiths and philosophies. But the Poverty Assassin was still present. It lived among them, doing what it always does. In those sad, violent countries it bred suspicion, violence, and hatred. It turned families and societies against each other. It kept people ignorant, robbed them of their health, stole their hopes and dreams, and often stopped them from dreaming at all. Instead, like so many people in my hometown, they'd come to assume that their nightmarish existence was the norm.

Again: it doesn't have to be this way.

We can pursue the Poverty Assassin, and exile him from our towns and neighborhoods. We can change minds, open hearts, and take action, putting him on the run. We can throw off his shackles, turn the tables, and take him off our streets. An individual can win the fight against poverty in his or her own life and family. We can join together in our neighborhoods and towns, acting through our schools, churches, businesses, and public institutions. We can stop this vicious assassin, heal the wounds he's inflicted, and keep him outside our borders. We can do this by helping ourselves, and ultimately by helping each other. We can face the task, educate ourselves, find jobs, become entrepreneurs, and finally kill this dogged criminal. That's what this book is about.

In March of 1929 a Republican President, Herbert Hoover, told this nation that the defeat of the Poverty Assassin was at hand. It was the end of the Roaring Twenties, and the country seemed richer than it ever had been—the wealthiest nation in all history. President Hoover felt that there must be a way to deploy some fraction of this abundance in an effort to lift all of the assassin's victims into lives free of want and hunger. The president's solution included some government encouragement but relied mainly on private enterprise and its seemingly ever-growing profits. Just months after he made this proposal, the Great Crash of 1929 sent Wall Street and Main Street into a steep downward spiral, followed by what's still regarded as the worst depression in history. Thirty-five years later, in the midst of the huge economic boom of the 1960s, a Democratic president, Lyndon Johnson, famously made a declaration of war against the Poverty Assassin. A flurry of new laws and government programs aimed at creating a comprehensive policy designed to solve all of society's ills. Innovative approaches to age-old problems targeted the effects of the Poverty Assassin in housing, education, health, and welfare. Johnson's war was massive and well-meaning, but most of it failed. Historians and economists debate the reasons for this failure to this very day, but the fact remains: Mr. Johnson lost his war.

As I write this, our nation is still emerging from the worst economic crisis since that of the 1930s. During this calamity, our ever-present poor have gotten even poorer. Families long accustomed to lifestyles in the middle class have fallen victim to the assassin's assaults, enduring wave after wave of foreclosures, bankruptcies, and lost jobs. As our economy recovers, some politician will again propose a nationwide effort to end this assassin's reign of terror for good. Obviously, this noble cause is also popular. While taxpayers are always reluctant to part with their hard-earned dollars, most know the fear of impoverishment too well, and they want it gone for good. Many are again ready for an all-out war.

This book is about an approach that might seem more modest. In a sense, it is. I'm not suggesting action by the national government, or by some consortium of our biggest corporations. I'll leave those possibilities for another time. I'm thinking more about what each of us can do in our homes, and in the world right outside our door.

In this approach, every individual is his or her own human capital, ready for investment in our combined future. That means each of you is a resource. Your unique talents and abilities can enable you to climb out of the Poverty Assassin's clutches. You can find a job, or even create one. You can learn the arts of entrepreneurship, and begin a business aimed at serving others as it turns a profit. Starting with your individual human capital (yourself), you can make use of your community's resources, and build a new and prosperous life. If you already have a good job or run a successful business, this book can help you understand the problems caused by the Poverty Assassin's inroads. It will go on to show you how to become a part of the solution. Either way, my approach is meant to create bonds between haves and have-nots so that we can all work together as a community. As we examine ways each individual can escape the stranglehold of this assassin, we will learn how to tap into a community's capacity (people, businesses, institutions, and infrastructure) so that every citizen can join in this effort.

Businesses, nonprofits, governments, churches, and schools are all a part of this process. Rich, poor, and those in between all have a stake in the outcome. All are a part of the social fabric, and all have an interest in making the community stronger. Though each of us has a different role to play in these efforts, the principles behind it remain the same. We must believe in ourselves, and in each other. Each of us owes it to himself or herself, to begin with individual action in the campaign to defeat this ugly killer of bodies and souls. Once we've taken that to heart, we must learn how to use our unique talents, individually and together, to contribute to the efforts of the community. We are all human capital. Each of us is a potential resource in our community's capacity to banish the Poverty Assassin from its borders.

It starts when we believe in ourselves and each other. It starts right here, with you. It has the potential to end in a bright new day for us all!

GLOBAL STRATIFICATION

R iches are relative. If you have absolutely nothing, someone who has a few dollars might seem like a billionaire. By the same principle, if you have a million dollars, and own a comfortable, middle-class home, but you live in an area full of vast estates that really are owned by billionaires, you will probably feel poor. That's one reason so many middle-income Americans think of themselves as being far poorer than they really are. By the world's standards, they are in the top few percentages, but compared to other Americans, they are average.

The World Bank publishes a map showing average income levels nation-by-nation around the globe. At a glance, it's easy to see who's rich and who's poor.

There are a few surprises. Upper North America, Japan, and Western Europe are still the largest pockets of the greatest riches on Earth. That's where the money is. A few other isolated spots do well, including Australia, South Korea, Israel, and Kuwait. When compared to those places, almost every other country in the world is poor. This is even true in the swiftly emerging economies of China and India. Those nations might join us at the top one day soon, but the vast majority of their people—the largest populations on the planet—are still mired in quicksand traps set by the Poverty Assassin.

Riches are relative here in America too. Though most of us are wealthy by global standards, when we look at one another, we find a few of those billionaires on one end and millions of people with nothing on the other. If you're homeless, broke, and hungry, a rented room with a hotplate and bath will feel like the lap of luxury. But if you arrive in that room after losing your house in foreclosure, you know you're bleeding from wounds you received from the Poverty Assassin.

We live in a world where the financial and material gap between haves and have-nots is growing. As the old cliché says: the rich get richer, and the poor get poorer. This has been particularly true in the U.S. for the past three decades, but it's also been true of our global economy.

Increasingly the world's nations and people find themselves on the extremes of "haves" and "have-nots." Though the "haves" include the very rich, far more of them are people who see themselves as earning average incomes. Many of these people own homes, cars, and have an adequate pension and health plans. Because they seldom come face-to-face with poverty, many middle-class people don't realize how much they have. This chapter will look at the Poverty Assassin's effects here in the U.S., and throughout the world, examining how peoples' economic status governs where and how they are born, live, and die. It will show how economics, the law, and other factors allow the rich to go through life without confronting the truth about the Poverty Assassin, while the poor must confront his onslaughts head-on every day.

The chasm between the rich and poor seems resistant to every equalizer. Programs promoting education, food and land redistribution, welfare, and health have all been marked by similar failures. Poverty resists them, and sometimes even feeds on them. On the other end, if a government tries to raise taxes too high, the rich pull their money out of that nation's economy, shifting it to the world's tax havens, such as Switzerland or the banks of the Cayman Islands. Once the money is hidden in another country, it's much harder to tax. Most governments don't even try. This often results in the poor and middle-class paying higher tax rates than their rich neighbors.

Statistics put this in stark relief: 50% of the world's people live on less than $2.50 per day, and own nothing; the top 1% own 40% of the world's assets. The three richest people on the planet own more assets between them than the poorest forty-eight nations combined. The long-term nature of rich-versus-poor in the U.S. can be best appreciated by looking at the last quarter of the twentieth century. In those years America's top fifth of all wage and salary earners saw their incomes skyrocket by 43% in constant dollars, while the poorest fifth saw theirs sink by 9%. Let's look at that in dollar amounts we can understand: If you were an average earner in the top 20%, and you made in constant dollars $100,000 per year in 1975, by the year 2000, your annual pay would rise to $143,000. But if you began 1975 with a yearly income of $10,000, by 2000, you would have seen that sink to $9,100.

These numbers show that every year, an average middle-class American is a little more likely to fall victim to the Poverty Assassin, and a little less likely to strike it rich. This makes the American Dream more and more distant to any normal wage earner. This growing inequality breeds discontent, crime, and even civil unrest. That's bad news for all of us, even the rich.

Some argue that the government should take up the slack, but that's less and less likely. With growing debt, lack of consensus, and a still-unstable economic picture, federal and state governments can do little but nibble around the edges of the problem. But that doesn't mean we should simply sit on our hands.

Take Robert, who comes from an impoverished family in a low-income inner-city neighborhood, and Douglas, who grew up in America's suburban middle class. Each grew up as an only child; each is forty years old. Robert's father left the family before Robert can remember. His mom has always worked whatever jobs she could find, but as a high school dropout, her options were limited. She'd been a maid, a ticket taker, and a waitress in inexpensive diners. She'd averaged about four months of unemployment each year. This wasn't because she didn't want to work. It was simply the unpredictable nature of the jobs she was qualified to do. In current dollars, Robert's mom was earning an average of about $14,000 per year. One year she earned only half that much, and in her best year, she brought home less than $20,000. Just a few miles away, in a neighborhood that was so different that it might have been on another planet, Doug's parents had a combined annual income of about $80,000.

They both turned eighteen in 1992. Both boys had done well in high school, and both wanted to go to college. Doug had gone to a "good" public suburban high school where virtually every student was expected to go to college. The only question was whether Doug could get into the schools he really wanted. He put in applications at five colleges and universities, with Johns Hopkins topping the list. Also among them were the University of Pennsylvania, two prestigious small colleges, and finally, just in case no one else took him, he filled one out for his state's university. Together the applications cost him what would be about $250 today. When the answers came back, he'd made it into all but one of the schools. There was no problem with his credentials, but one of the small colleges had run out of space.

Though Doug had thought of Hopkins as his first choice, that altered with changing circumstances. Hopkins had the highest tuition and offered the least financial aid. Though Doug came from a comfortable home, and his parents had saved some money, all four schools that accepted him offered some kind of aid package. With tuition, room, and board at the private schools running at about $25,000 per year in the early 1990s, full price at any one of them would have been more than his parents could pay. His state school was considerably less, but that would've been his last choice.

Doug finally settled on the University of Pennsylvania's Business program where two-thirds of his costs would be covered. His parents' contribution, supplemented by $5,000 per year in low-interest student loans, allowed him to go there without mortgaging too much of his future. He went through in four years, earning a bachelor's degree. After graduation, he spent five nervous months looking for a job, but finally found what he wanted. He went to work in an executive training program at a local bank. They paid for him to get a master's degree in Finance, then he earned several promotions. Doug is now a vice president in charge of the bank's small business division. He paid back his student loan long ago. Doug and his wife, Genevieve (a small business owner with twelve employees), have paid off the mortgage on a $500,000 home, have a net worth of just above $2 million, and their combined earnings come to over $300,000 per year.

The same year Doug was applying to some of the top schools in the country, Robert put in three applications. Like Robert, he sent one to his state university. The other two were local community colleges. He might've applied to others, but he saw no reason to fill out and pay for applications to schools he couldn't afford. When Robert investigated student aid packages, he found he was limited because of his record in high school. Though he'd graduated with honors, some of his courses weren't college prep. This was typical at his inner-city school. The school's core program aimed at helping its students learn trades. Few of his classmates gave four-year colleges much thought. The majority didn't go to college and most of those who did wound up in two-year community college programs.

Though the state university accepted Robert, in the end, he couldn't go there. He qualified for a partial scholarship, an on-campus job, and a student loan, but he would've still needed to come up with at least $3,500 per semester, or $7,000 per year. The money simply couldn't be found. Instead, he took classes at a community college. Going part-time, he got his Associate's degree in four years. A year after graduation, he was still working part-time and living with his mom. That's when he finally got a full-time job with the County Department of Parks & Recreation. Eighteen years later he manages a park maintenance crew of four and earns $32,000 per year. His wife, Amy, does temp work and earns about a third of that. They have two children: an eight-year-old boy and a six-year-old girl. They are buying the tiny house they live in. The price was $80,000. They've paid off the first four years of a thirty-year mortgage.

Like most Americans, both Robert and Doug think of themselves as middle-class citizens with middle-class families. Both would describe the conditions they grew up in as modest. Though both men would agree that there have been disappointments, each sees himself as doing reasonably well. If we were to talk to either of these men about his lot in life, without any mention of numbers, addresses, or specific schools, their stories might sound quite similar. Yet, as we can already see, the differences were, and are, huge.

Robert started life in a family with an income in the bottom fifth among American households. Doug's family was in the top quarter. Robert struggled and studied, going further in school than anyone in his family had before. So did Doug, but he advanced much further than Robert. Twenty years after their high school graduations, Robert has barely managed to pull himself up a rung. His family is still in the bottom half of the earnings scale, but he's slowly nearing the middle. Doug's family has risen to the upper 2%. As long as Doug's kids' academic records are good enough, they can go to any school they want. He and his wife included that in their long-term budget years ago. Robert's children have the same resources he had—practically none. They face a harsh educational environment with rising costs and shrinking opportunities.

This is how the rich get richer, and the poor get poorer. It's also the truth behind our illusions of where we fit into our world. If one of Robert's kids gets a full scholarship to Harvard, it will make his whole family feel richer. If Doug and his wife suffer some financial reverses, losing half a million dollars in net worth, and $100,000 per year in income, they will feel poor. Yet that still leaves them with income and riches that Robert and his family can't even imagine.

More and more of us live in families like Robert's, while the number of Dougs in the world stays about the same, causing their percentage to shrink. The Poverty Assassin takes aim at the working poor. They're such easy targets. The number of rich doesn't shrink, but it doesn't grow much either. Most population growth—both nationally and worldwide—is among the poor.

All of this depends on comparative environments. If Robert's family had the same income but lived in a Third World nation, they would seem as wealthy within their society as Doug and his family are here. Robert's children would have opportunities and privileges that their impoverished classmates could only dream about. If Doug and his family lived in that

Third World country, they would seem almost impossibly rich.

Wealth and poverty are relative terms, but almost all of us want wealth. We correctly see wealth as the key to personal freedom. Poverty is prison. Poverty is slavery. Poverty is the assassin of happiness and dreams. If we are ever going to guarantee freedom and opportunity for every American, we must stop this assassin in its tracks.

A Game Theory Perspective: What We Give for What We Need

Game theory uses math, logic, and psychology to explain how people interact with each other in situations where they have something at stake. It tries to explain why people make the choices they do. A game theoretician looks at human interactions, and asks: What does each person want? What will he or she do to get it? Why does one set of decisions lead to success, while another ends in failure? Game theory helps us understand motivations and behaviors in finance, politics, economics, psychology, military conflicts, or almost any other field where we make decisions affecting others.

Game theory doesn't work without people. If the theory is going to function, at least two people (seen as "players") must interact with one another. Each player wants something from the other; these desires often come into conflict with one another. Neither player can get all of what he or she wants unless the opposing player is exploited, controlled, or eliminated. If none of the players can gain complete control, then two or more of them must cooperate to find a solution—if there is a solution. This doesn't always happen. Sometimes games just turn into more games.

A signature game theory scenario is called: the Prisoner's Dilemma. In this situation, two players are held prisoner. Both have been arrested and accused of the same serious crime. We interrogate them in separate rooms, and they have no means to communicate. Each is totally ignorant of what the other is saying. If one confesses and the other stays silent, the player who's confessed goes free, while the one who keeps silent gets twenty years. If both players confess, they will each get ten years. To do this, they would have to confess simultaneously.

Obviously, each suspect considers confessing before the other does. Doing so would lead to one player's complete freedom. But if both confess at the same moment, they share the burden, splitting the jail time evenly. Most theoreticians assume the two will compete to confess first, but in doing so, they're likely to create circumstances where they are likely to confess at the same time. It doesn't matter whether these simultaneous confessions result from cooperation or competition; once they've simultaneously admitted their guilt, both players get the same sentences: ten years each.

One of the most common components in game theory situations is money. Money can give players power, security, and independence. In any financial dealings, a player would want to figure out: Who has how much? Who can get more from the other? In real life, this soon becomes complicated. Though there are financial situations that only involve two people, the effects of most money problems spill over into the lives of many players. When two families compete, all the family members have an interest. When several companies vie for the same market, executives, employees, and consumers are all in the mix. Each person has different goals, as does each organization or corporation.

Conflicts about money are often also about power. Whoever controls the funds gets to run things.

When we look at our fellow humans in terms of absolute necessities, we find that our needs are roughly equal. All of us must eat, drink, sleep, and find shelter. Without these, most of us won't survive long. After we've provided ourselves with these necessities, we consider our acquired needs—modern conveniences we've integrated into our lives so completely that living without them has become unimaginable. Something is an acquired need when society has elevated it to the status of a basic necessity. Without it, one might survive, but that person can't fully participate in the life of the community.

Most of our acquired needs develop out of technology. For instance, indoor plumbing and central heating weren't basic parts of most American homes until about a hundred years ago. Even in the cold northern winters, most people got along with fireplaces, coal stoves, and outhouses. But once indoor plumbing arrived, people found they couldn't live without it. They also soon realized that if they had to have running water indoors, the heat was an absolute must. Without it, pipes would freeze and burst during every cold snap. Soon central heat was everywhere, making indoor plumbing possible year-round. In a few short years, both conveniences became necessities. Renters and buyers alike demanded them. Lawmakers required both utilities in building and housing codes. Courts ruled that landlords must provide them in all rental units. In recent years the same thing has happened with air conditioning. Many governments require it in all publicly funded facilities. In the southern U.S., many communities have ruled air conditioning to be a necessity.

Heat, air conditioning, and most other modern technologies depend on energy. With our current systems and resources, our energy supply is finite. We can only produce so much of it. That's why we spend so much time, money, and political capital to get it. A century ago, when the developed Western nations began competing for fossil fuels in the oil-rich Middle East, their conflicts were often labeled: The Great Game. Wherever these nations found easily accessible oil fields, they began to play. Each tried to buy off local leaders, and influence public affairs. Private oil companies got into the game and sometimes came into conflict with their own governments. The players fought wars, shaped peace settlements, and dictated economic policies. We've continued that competition right up to the present.

Using the lens of game theory, the competition for energy looks something like this: Scientists discover an energy source in a poor nation. Rich nations and their corporations swoop in. Each rich nation has its own supply of money, political prestige, and military power. The poor nation has the actual resource but lacks any other tools to force a conclusion to the game. The impoverished nation has no money, armaments, or any other basic tools of power politics. If this nation is going to have any voice in its future, it must depend on diplomacy and international law. These feeble crutches seldom get a player off the sidelines. Instead, they must sit on the bench while other players decide their fate.

If powerful nations have a great enough need for energy, the poor, powerless nation's claim to the resources within its borders becomes shaky. The weak nation's lone hope is to manipulate its more powerful neighbors to compete to fulfill its needs. The goals are almost always the same. Get these rich nations to come in and start schools. Let them create banks and develop new industries. For the poor nation's people, these are essential to progress. They must trade their resources for technological advances, but as long as there are profits for everyone, the poor nation's government retains control. If the poor nation can't live with its more powerful neighbors, one or more of them will try to take the resource by force. The poor nation might avoid this by inviting the powerful nations in and giving them attractive ways to get what they want. These attractive methods can be designed to produce side effects that benefit the poor nation.

The same principles apply to individual interactions.

Game theory provides a model for the dynamics of international power, but how well does it work in our mundane day-to-day lives? Do we have the power to get what we want? With whom are we competing? Do we have potential allies who might cooperate with us?

Game theory in microcosm: A neighborhood parking policy

A few months ago, when Janet Middleton bought her townhouse, she liked almost everything about it. She liked that it had plenty of space inside, but just a small, private backyard patio outside. She always liked the idea of owning a home, but she'd always dreaded the upkeep on a lawn and garden. With this place, there wasn't a single blade of grass to mow—just bricks that could be easily hosed off. She liked the way her sunporch was set up to be an office and the efficient use of every inch of kitchen space.

Like many row homes, this one was only about fifteen feet wide, and its lot was the same width as the house. It didn't have a garage or carport. The only parking was out on the street. Janet's car was a Nissan Pathfinder, which was almost sixteen feet long. When parking, even if she centered it perfectly, it stretched a few inches beyond the property lines on both ends of her lot. Janet doubted that this would be a problem.

Her new next-door neighbor, Fred, had a different opinion.

"Are you living here?" he asked the morning after she'd moved in. He'd just come outside to get his newspaper.

"Yes. I'm Janet Middleton," she said, extending her hand in a friendly greeting.

"Fred Knot," he said coolly, shaking her hand as if it were an unwanted obligation. He released her fingers and glanced beyond her to her car. He walked up and down, concentrating on the front and rear bumpers. "Too long," he said.

"Excuse me?"

"Your car's too long for your space. Each of us gets fifteen feet. That's the width of each lot. But just about everybody around here tries to hog a lot more than that. One car, two cars, trucks, SUVs . . . all these folks move in here from the 'burbs, and they all think they can park anything anywhere. My guess is, that describes you."

"What do you mean?"

"Grew up in the 'burbs. You're used to a big lot, a driveway, and probably a garage, too—plenty of parking for a two- or three- or even a four-car family. You move into the city, where the lot's fifteen feet wide instead of a hundred — no driveway, carport, or garage. Just a street jammed with more parked cars than it was ever meant to handle. It's folks like you that made this happen, but I'm not letting it go on. Your rear bumper's right on your southern property line— just makes it."

"So you're not going after me," Janet said, watching her new neighbor for confirmation.

Fred eyed her. "If I weren't going after you, I wouldn't be out here talking to you. You're new. I've been here all my life—inherited the house from my parents. You don't know how things work around here, but you'll learn." He walked to the front bumper.

"See," he said, pointing to the sidewalk. "Your lot ends here, but your car's front end extends past that, crossing about a foot into my space. You can leave it there for now, but, in the future, I'd suggest you make some other arrangement."

"What other arrangement?" Janet demanded. "There's an empty space in front of my house. My car fits here, so I park it here."

"Right! And you take up some of my space," Fred countered. "You can either back up, and use some of your other neighbor's parking space, or you can park in one of the off-street lots nearby."

"I looked," said Janet. "The nearest one is a ten-minute walk, and it costs $15 per day."

"That's one of the drawbacks of city living," said Fred. "You could always get a smaller car." Fred smiled, picked up his newspaper from the sidewalk, and went back into his house. Janet watched him, wondering if he was serious.

Later that day she met other neighbors who'd known Fred for a while. "You can bet he's serious," said Cindy, who lived across the street. "Parking's at a premium around here, and some people go way overboard about it. Fred's one of them. He's retired, with a really nice pension, which means he's got lots of time on his hands. He uses it to be the neighborhood's parking monitor. If he thinks you're taking his space, he'll look for any way he can to get you towed."

"He can't dictate on-street parking!" Janet exclaimed.

"No, but he can try."

In the following days, Janet did all she could to comply with Fred's wishes. Then came a late night when the only space on her block stretched across several feet of pavement in front of his house. When she parked there, she found a note on her windshield the next morning. "Further use of this space will be at your own risk," Fred had written.

Two days later, she parked there again. When she didn't get a note, she thought he'd given up. Not long after that, she came home one night, and parked down the block, not far from the fire hydrant. She estimated the distance and decided she was probably far enough away to avoid a ticket. When she came out the next morning, her car was gone—towed to a garage that charged her $300.

After she'd paid, gotten her car, and cooled her initial anger, she talked with Cindy about her options. "He certainly knows how to use the law to his advantage," said Janet.

"Sure, but only if you've agreed to play his game," Cindy replied. "He's assuming he'll be the one enforcing the rules. You're the one who's going to break them. As long as you accept your role, he'll have you at a disadvantage."

"Then, what should I do?" Janet asked. "I've thought of doing the same thing to him, but I don't even know what kind of car he has."

"An old VW," said Cindy. "He keeps it in the basement lot of an apartment building a few blocks from here. A friend owns the building and lets Fred park for free. You won't get him on that."

"Why does he do this?" Janet wondered.

"Because it's the one thing he has left. Fred was a legislative librarian at City Hall. Sounds dull, but to him the job was everything. Then he hit sixty-five and had to retire. He doesn't work, has no hobbies, and he's not interested in sports. This is the one place left where he can actually affect other people's lives, and he's determined to do it."

"He likes the power," Janet observed.

"Exactly."

Janet thought about that for a moment, then said: "If it's power he wants, maybe we should give it to him."

"I don't follow."

"Parking's always an issue in this neighborhood. Does that mean the neighborhood association has a parking policy?"

Cindy nodded. "More like ten or twenty policies. They've tried to come up with something that applies to the whole neighborhood, but no one can ever agree. So our parking policy changes with every block."

"When's the association's next meeting?" Janet asked.

"Next week."

"Will he be there?"

"Most likely. I've never known him to miss one."

Janet used the following days to study the neighborhood's parking situation. The problem was simple and familiar: too many cars and too little space. The details could be incredibly complicated. There were parking rules aimed at employees of local businesses, more rules for their customers, and a parking policy for the staff at a nearby elementary school. Two through-streets banned parking during rush hours, morning and evening. Three churches attracted congregants from throughout the city, but only one had a parking lot, and it was tiny.

Janet wrote up a resolution she would introduce at the meeting. It called for a parking policy favoring residents, but sensitive to everyone's needs. It required that policy to be comprehensive. Though it gave no other details, it did list one more requirement: that any dispute between neighbors should be settled by those neighbors. According to her resolution, all neighborhood parking rules would encourage neighbors to solve their disputes with a minimum of legal complaints or actions.

But the most vital part of Janet's proposal was the committee. She suggested that there be a permanent panel made up of five people nominated and confirmed by the association's entire membership. Heading the committee would be the job of its chairperson. Whoever accepted this position would give up the right to propose changes. The chairperson would move the committee's work along, preside over the votes, and work with city officials on traffic ordinances. Proposed changes would require a unanimous vote of the committee, confirmed by a two-thirds vote of the residents. The chairperson would have to persuade most of the neighborhood residents before any changes could be made.

Finally, Janet's proposal contained her own nomination for the chair's job: Fred.

"But why?" Cindy asked.

"Because it's his favorite subject," Janet said. "Because he's an expert. And because it will force him to take everyone's concerns into consideration. As you said, I was playing his game. So did everybody else. We kept losing, right?"

"Right," said Cindy.

"So now we stop fighting and let him win. He'll be the go-to guy for all parking issues. We give him all the responsibility, but keep all the power in the hands of the association. He'll start out by thinking like a dictator. He'll assume he can make things go the way he wants them to. But in no time he'll be dealing with so many little parking fights that he won't be able to keep up with it. That's when he'll discover that he doesn't have the power to solve them. All he'll be able to do is suggest solutions. If he doesn't come up with good ones, he'll be discredited on the issue that concerns him most. If he leads the committee to a sensible policy we all can accept, then he'll have to accept it too. But by that time, it'll be his proposal, so he'll want to."

"How crafty," Cindy said, grinning.

"Not really. I'm just making him play my game," Janet replied.

When Fred was first appointed chairperson, he was thrilled. Once he got into the actual work, he was horrified at his own impotence. As the weeks passed, he often felt frustrated, but he couldn't quit. He pushed his committee until they came up with a policy acceptable to the entire neighborhood. He disliked many of the details but was barred from making changes by the terms of his job. When his neighbors praised the proposed policy, he began to like the sound of it. By the time of the vote, he was half-convinced that he'd engineered the proposal himself.

Moments after the proposal passed, Janet congratulated Fred, saying: "Don't you think you've changed?"

Fred smiled. "Of course I have. Your proposal is my proposal now. I've learned to play your game. All you have to worry about is what I'm going to do with it."

Janet thought about that for a moment, then grinned at him. Both knew their game was just beginning.

POVERTY AS A NEOCLASSICAL MODEL

O ne of the basics of neoclassical economics is the theory of supply and demand. This is the idea that price fluctuations are governed by the amount of a particular product or service available (supply), and consumers' need for that product or service (demand). If there's more supply than demand, the price goes down. If there's a shortage of the product or service, the price goes up. For example, if we have one hundred light bulbs, and one hundred users of light bulbs and each user is willing to spend a dollar for electric light, then each light bulb will cost a dollar. However, if there are only fifty light bulbs, and all one hundred users want one, the light bulb provider will see an opportunity to get $2 per bulb. If he sells all fifty for the $2 price, that means the smaller supply has created greater demand, a higher price, with higher profit, and, for those who can't or won't spend $2, a shortage. This process creates prices that are in "equilibrium" between the supply of a product or service and the demand for it. The provider then liquidates the supply of the commodity at the price consumers are willing to pay. If some potential consumers go without due to lack of funds, that proves the theory works. In strict supply-and-demand models, products and services go where the money is. Those without funds get nothing.

But what happens when many people need something badly, but the limited supply drives the price up beyond their means? Or what if the cost of producing and distributing the product or service is more than consumers can pay? Then they have to go without. Victims of the Poverty Assassin are often in this position. Almost everything we need costs money.

What happens when we don't have it? If you have no money at all, any price is too high.

Poverty's most visible victims are the homeless. Most homeless people own nothing beyond the clothes they're wearing. They have only as much money as they can beg, borrow, or steal, then carry with them. Whatever they get, they spend right away. They usually have to, and cash is a target for thieves. The homeless lack bank accounts, property, or income. This often makes cash into more of a problem than a solution.

Serena hit bottom when she was still a teenager. She'd never known her father, and her mom was a heroin addict. Through most of Serena's childhood, her mom usually managed to put a roof over their heads, and buy food. Serena was smart, liked school, and dreamt of going to college. In an attempt to make that dream possible, Serena's mom started selling heroin on the street. It was the only road she knew to real money. She saved over $2,000 before they caught her. She'd been shoplifting candy bars from the drugstore where Serena worked after school. She'd had enough heroin in her possession to make an "intent to distribute" charge automatic. The $2,000 paid her lawyer fees, but she still wound up with a three-year prison sentence. That left sixteen-year-old Serena broke, homeless, and even jobless. Her mother's attempted theft had gotten her fired.

Serena's first need was a home. Her state's social services network of institutions and foster families didn't appeal to her at all. She would be eighteen soon enough and figured if she could survive on her own until then, she would be all right. She'd endured nights of homelessness with her mother, and already had the necessary skills to live on the street. When she found the sheriff's notice on their apartment door, she started packing. She knew what to take and what to leave. She didn't bother with sentimentality; she couldn't afford it. She would've tried a shelter, but she'd gone that route with her mom more than once. Their stays in those places had convinced Serena that the street was the lesser evil.

Most of her town's homeless people eventually took up residence in encampments beneath one of two interstate overpasses. One of these camps was home to pedophiles, rapists, and other violent criminals. The other was populated mostly by drug addicts, alcoholics, and children. Serena went to that one. She'd once spent a single night there with her mother. She arrived with a backpack, sleeping bag, two bags of trail mix, a full water bottle and $28. She found a relatively safe-looking space that had just been vacated and started setting up.

As she laid out her sleeping bag, a little boy came up. "You gotta pay ten bucks to the Boss Man," he said.

"What Boss Man?" she demanded.

The boy pointed to a bearded man about thirty yards away. "Him." The man was looking through a pile of blankets. An old woman had just stacked them on a rickety table. She was talking fast. Boss Man said nothing as he unfolded each blanket, then refolded and restacked them. Finally, she saw him reach under the table, and pull out a bottle of cheap wine. Once he'd exchanged a few words with the woman, she took the wine and left. One pile of blankets for one bottle of wine—supply-and-demand at work. This was the economics of homelessness.

Serena walked over to him. "I understand you run things around here," she said.

The bearded man stood up straight. He was about six-foot-six and was built like an NFL lineman. "Right," he said. "Name's Link, but most folks call me 'Boss Man.'"

"Because you're the boss," she said.

"That's right."

"That little boy over there said you want ten dollars from me."

"If you're gonna stay in that spot, that's what you gotta pay."

"Why ten?"

"That's what I decided," said Link.

"But what made you decide on ten?"

"Don't try none of that," he snarled. "It's ten whether you like it or not—and it's every week. If you don't have the $10, you have to bring something I need, or can trade. You do that; we'll get along."

Serena went back to her spot, crouched over, hiding her hands, and pretended to pull a $10 bill from her sleeping bag, when it was actually coming out of her pocket. She was familiar with the homeless practice of never putting your cash or valuables anywhere but on your person. Serena paid Link, who then explained the few rules he enforced: never cause trouble, bring all disputes to him, and never do anything that would bring the cops under the bridge.

Serena spent the first few days acclimating herself to the camp and its ways. She used the portable toilets at a nearby construction site when she had to, and showered in the gym at school. She soon realized how lucky she'd been to get the spot she had. Link operated his business on a first-come-first-served basis, and she'd just happened to find the newly vacated spot when she did. It was one of about a dozen $10 locations. These were the ones closest to Link, who had taken the best spot for himself. These were the highest, driest, safest locations in the area. He only charged $5 each week for the ones beyond. He made no guarantees for possessions, but he assured each tenant of having their spot each night and stopped anyone who wanted to bother those who were sleeping.

During the days Serena went up top, going beyond the overpass into the nearby neighborhoods. On one side was an old, deserted factory, and block after block of deteriorating row homes. Some houses were occupied, but others were boarded up. On the other side was a new industrial park. The streets surrounding it were lined with fast-food joints, car dealerships, and a couple of strip malls. Chain-link fences defined the borders on both sides. Each fence had a narrow entranceway connecting the makeshift homeless encampment with the surrounding neighborhood. Using bolt cutters, tenants had sliced several temporary gaps in both fences.

Serena went into each business, looking for a job. Everyone turned her down until she got to the fast-food restaurant. The manager didn't have any jobs in the restaurant, but before Serena left, another thought occurred to him.

"I don't know if it would interest you, but I'd pay someone $125 a week to clean up my parking lot each morning. It takes about an hour. It would still be over $100 after taxes."

"I'll take it," she said.

Working an hour each day was enough to keep her going. She could pay Link for her spot (one of the driest in the area), and buy just enough food to avoid the worst pangs of hunger. Every morning she left the parking lot spotless. Before the first week was over, her boss approached her.

"Some people around here have been looking for someone like you," he said. "Go talk to Yvonne at the Honda dealer. Her place might take longer, but you can charge her more. With that, and what I pay you, maybe we can find you a real place to live."

In the month it took her to reach that goal, Serena became a radical agent of change in the community beneath the overpass. Her work in the parking lots was so good, other business owners noticed. Soon they were lining up to hire her. "I can't clean up every lot," she told them. "I'm still in high school."

"Do you know anyone else who would do it?" asked the bank manager at one strip mall.

She thought about that, and said: "Maybe."

Though the business owners distrusted most of their homeless neighbors, they allowed them to do these outdoor chores as long as Serena was there to supervise them. She took on enough cleanup work to occupy a dozen of her fellow residents. Each day she woke them up, got them each a breakfast, and told them which lots they were cleaning. The owners paid her as they would a subcontractor, and she paid her neighbors out of that. After a month she could afford the rent for a small apartment. The owner of the fast-food place set it up for her, cosigning the lease.

Link helped her pack up her things. "I hope you ain't leaving for good."

"No way," said Serena. "All my employees are here. You'll see me every morning."

"Yeah, I guess that's good," said Link. "What would you think if I raised the rent around here a little bit. I think the nice spots like yours might be worth $15 a week. Just about all of them work for you, and now they're making money."

"If you can get it, I won't stop you," she said. "After all, you control what they want, and if they're willing to pay . . . "

Link grinned. "Supply and demand, right?"

"Exactly," said Serena. "But have you ever thought of doing what you do here, legally?"

"Legally?"

"Like maybe managing a building—renting rooms and apartments, doing maintenance, calling in repairmen… that stuff."

He scratched his head. "I guess I could."

"I might know a place that needs a super," she said.

"It's gotta be nearby," said Link, "if I'm gonna keep my thing goin' here."

"You don't understand. You would live there."

"What would an apartment cost?"

"Supply and demand usually rules that price, too," said Serena, "but your apartment would be rent-free as long as you did the work."

"I might be ready for that," he said, "and maybe some of our working neighbors are ready to live under a real roof instead of a highway interchange."

There, at the bottom of the financial ladder, Serena and Link were beginning their climb up the rungs. They'd both learned how supply and demand could help them lift themselves up, escaping the assaults of the Poverty Assassin. It would be a difficult journey, but they weren't going down this road alone. When you provide a lifeline, some poor, but hopeful people are always there to grab it.

Racial Inequality

Serena, Link, and most of their neighbors are African-Americans. Though plenty of homeless citizens are white, the Poverty Assassin's victims in urban areas tend to be black or members of some other minority. This is the sad truth about minorities today: the financial deck is stacked against them.

Some of this is due to the isolation of poverty. Poor people usually live together in the same neighborhoods. This isn't a choice. Where we live is dependent on what we can afford. The poor have little to spend on rent and real estate, so they go where the prices are low. This puts them directly in the sights of the Poverty Assassin.

This economic isolation has its roots in the segregation of the past. In the twentieth century, African-Americans moved north for jobs. For far too long they'd lived on a Jim Crow starvation diet dictated by the Poverty Assassin. As formerly enslaved blacks transformed themselves into sharecroppers on southern farms, they quickly learned that they had only exchanged one set of chains for another. Before the Civil War, they'd been bound to the land by the laws of slavery. Now they were imprisoned, often on the same plantations and farms, by the laws of economics. Whites allowed them to continue to work the fields in exchange for a share of the crop. In good years these "freed" people might break even. In bad years their debts to the landowners grew. With just a couple of poor crops, they would fall so far behind that they could never pay the landowners back. These landowners now had the same workforce they'd had when they were cotton barons, but they no longer had any legal responsibility for the welfare of those workers. African-Americans who wanted to leave were told they had to pay their debts first. Escaping these situations was often as dangerous as the flight of a runaway slave, but many people managed to do it. Many left for the promise of factory work in the North.

As African-Americans moved from the rural south to the northern industrial cities, many of the laws, traditions, and customs of racial segregation followed them. When it came to racial prejudice, northern whites were not very different from their southern counterparts. They didn't want black folks next door, in their children's classroom, or at work. When African-Americans moved into a neighborhood, whites moved out. Once a school allowed a token black in the front door, whites started exiting out the back. Whole sections of large cities went from all-white to all-black almost overnight.

Though northern jobs paid better, the money was seldom enough to break the Poverty Assassin's stranglehold. Factories hired African-Americans to sweep floors, and paid them a minimum wage. White housewives paid even less when they hired black women to do the cooking and cleaning. The North's segregation was more isolating than the South's. Whatever the pitfalls, in the South, the lives of whites and blacks intersected in all kinds of circumstances. In the North, when the workday was over, African-Americans were expected to return to their neighborhoods where their lives seldom touched those of whites.

When African-Americans started doing work that required skill, whites denied them the credentials and benefits that went with those better job descriptions. A maid would soon be managing an entire household, or a janitor would be doing carpentry and plumbing, with no change in pay, or job status. This kept them in the same neighborhoods, where they suffered from the same indignities and hopelessness that they always had.

Generations have passed, and though the United States has made progress on race in the legal, social, and cultural spheres, many of America's poor people of color have been left behind. Despite their advances, African-Americans, and other minorities are increasingly likely to be shunted into high-poverty neighborhoods. These neighborhoods are becoming more and more limited and isolated. They are limited to the poor and isolated from the mainstream by their economic status. It's a form of segregation that begins with race and gets reinforced by poverty.

When poverty takes over, poor children attend school with other poor children. After school, they go home to poor neighborhoods. Most of the adults they see every day are poor. Only the police, teachers, and storeowners regularly earn middle- income wages, and they all go back to their homes in better areas as soon as their shifts are over.

Kids living in a neighborhood like this find few legitimately successful role models, if any. Many of their potential role models are people who reject them. Henry is a ten-year-old African-American boy in a typical, unnamed neighborhood in Detroit, a city whose impoverished population is served by a government that's struggling with bankruptcy. Henry likes to visit Mr. Marsh's convenience store and Ms. Gomez's candy store, but neither of those white proprietors likes to see him coming. After two stick-ups, Mr. Marsh has put his cash register behind a bulletproof façade, while Ms. Gomez keeps a loaded gun behind her counter. Both see every young customer as a potential thief.

When Henry goes to school, it's not much different. His fifth-grade teacher, Mrs. Manion, can barely keep her students in the classroom. For every hour in class, she spends twenty minutes teaching, and forty minutes getting the kids to keep quiet. She often sends unruly students to the vice principal's office, if only to get rid of them. Though Henry is a good kid, he sits among a half dozen homeboys who like to act up. When they all start yelling and punching each other, Mrs. Manion sends all the boys in the section to see the vice principal. That includes Henry. Once, when his classmates were suspended, he was too.

Sometimes when Henry is walking home, he gets stopped by Officer Thomas of Detroit's PD. Once, when Henry was in Ms. Gomez's candy store, three other boys came in and started pocketing candy bars and other items. When Ms. Gomez saw Officer Thomas's police cruiser stopping at the intersection, she ran out and called to him. The three boys ran. Thomas got two of them and took Henry in as well. Henry managed to get off with a warning from a police sergeant, but since then Thomas stops him regularly, questioning him as if he were a suspect.

Officer Thomas, Ms. Gomez, and Mr. Marsh all live in white working-class suburbs. Mrs. Manion and the vice principal are African-American, but neither of them lives within the city limits anymore. They've escaped the Poverty Assassin's stigma. Henry's family hasn't.

Henry's mother waits tables at a neighborhood diner. Most of the clientele is poor, and her tips aren't much. Henry's father was killed in Iraq not long after Henry was born.

When Henry walks around his neighborhood, he sees white entrepreneurs who are afraid of him. Most of the black entrepreneurs he sees are drug dealers, prostitutes, and pimps. He doesn't have to ask why. These illegal entrepreneurs look at a kid like Henry and assume he'll be working for them one day. The white business owners make the same assumption. They won't hire him. It would never occur to the whites to offer a neighborhood kid like Henry a job. They prefer to keep jobs in the family, or at least within their race.

In vast areas of Detroit and other cities, whites see all black kids as potential thieves. Young African-Americans see only what the Poverty Assassin has left them: dilapidated buildings, boarded-up storefronts, and playgrounds that look more like fields of bombed-out rubble. The only obvious routes to financial success seem to be drug dealing or related criminal activities. Those of us with advantages must lead the way in changing all this. We must identify the problems racism causes, and find effective solutions. We must expose our young people to successful mentors at the earliest possible moment. We must show them how to dodge the Poverty Assassin's bullets, and find legitimate financial success.

HOUSING & COMMUNITY DEVELOPMENT

O ne of the first and most obvious indicators of a person's well-being is the place where that person lives. Our homes are often the best barometers of our financial health. For the rich, "home" might be a luxury penthouse or a vast country estate. For victims of the Poverty Assassin, it could be an informal encampment beneath an interstate overpass, like the one where Serena settled in Chapter 4. In Chapter 3, Janet, Cindy, and Fred are among the more comfortable "middle class" whose modest homes fall between these two extremes. Nonetheless, these "modest" homes provide their single owners with a lot of living space.

Americans prefer homes with a lot of space. Among people in developed nations, only Australians have more. Our homes average 2,170 square feet, while our friends down under don't feel comfortable without an extra 140 square feet, bringing their average up to 2,310. The average British subject manages to get through his or her days within the confines of 818 square feet. In the developed world, space equals money. That's true in the price of the house, but even more in the price of its upkeep.

A big house requires more heating, cooling, lighting, cleaning, and maintenance. Janet could get the exterior of her small row house painted for less than $1,500, but the owner of a suburban McMansion might spend $6,000 or more for the same service.

In the West, home ownership has become a sign of affluence and responsibility. Many young people find that it's the first investment others advise them to make. Homeownership roots people within a community, and encourages the creation and growth of new families.

In America, we've developed mythical ideas about houses and homes. In earlier times, when America was populated mostly by farmers, the family farm took on an almost mystical meaning. Like our modern houses today, those family farms were far bigger than the ones in other parts of the world. Many early immigrants left behind holdings of ten acres or less, only to settle on sections here that were twenty or even fifty times bigger.

Later, when Americans left their farms for the city, they often moved into overcrowded, unsanitary tenements. However, as they found work, and made a little money, they escaped those places, moving to more comfortable quarters. Inevitably they gravitated toward more spacious homes. A row home like Janet's might sit on a lot no bigger than the house's footprint (750 square feet), but this gets multiplied by two or three floors, and usually a basement. A tiny urban lot might have a home with twice as much floor area as the farmhouse where the occupants previously lived.

Compared to most of the world's people, the average American lives in a luxurious home. The American has indoor plumbing, electricity, comfortable furniture, refrigerator, washer-dryer, TV, a computer, and other home entertainments and luxuries. Compare this to the billion world citizens at the bottom of the economic ladder. They sleep beneath leaky roofs (if they have any shelter at all), without access to potable water, electricity, communications, or long-term security. What little clothing they have is unwashed and ragged. Almost all are illiterate, with little or no hope of getting an education. When these people have children, their only realistic expectation for their offspring is a life just as miserable as their own.

But this problem doesn't stop outside our borders. In 2009 there were over six hundred thousand chronically homeless people in the U.S. Over one and a half million Americans spent a period of time in homeless shelters that year. For some, these shelters were the places where they finally hit bottom. Their once-prosperous lives had spiraled into failure and defeat, and, lacking other resources, or constrained by embarrassment and pride, they needed to make use of this emergency service. Often the experience scares them. Though some shelters have the capability of providing real comfort, most are understaffed, underfunded, and too small to meet the needs of their occupants. Many onetime users depart in the morning, determined never to go this route again. Most of the chronically homeless only use shelters during the worst heat waves and during blizzards and freezing weather.

Societies are made up of people and the lives they live. A society's survival depends on its ability to provide the basic building blocks for the kind of lives people want. Beyond food and clothing, our primary need is shelter. We need a safe, permanent structure that we can call home. This is a community's most basic requirement: sheltered places where residents can eat, sleep, relax, and feel secure.

In most undeveloped nations, the surface meaning of "home" hasn't changed in centuries. People live in small villages, some coastal, and others on the edges of cultivated fields. Individuals and families live in huts, tepees, or other small, traditional structures. They live with far fewer necessities than we do. To them, indoor plumbing is an impossible dream. Electricity is a fascinating resource with great potential, but they've never had it in their homes. TV, radio, phone, and Internet are items they've heard about, and perhaps even seen, but none of these miracles has a place in their huts, or even in the village. The nearest electrical lines are often miles away. Nevertheless, those carriers of electricity influence people in the remote village, if only because the people dream of what they would do if electric power suddenly appeared in their lives.

That's the surface of the idea of "home," but if we dig down, we find this idea has altered in almost invisible ways. Today the world holds far more of these communities, and a lot of villages have many more residents than they ever did before. These new occupants eat the village's food, drink its water, and build more huts, or other abodes, around its now-sprawling edges. Why? A few aspects of modern life have actually reached them.

National and international aid efforts have brought new benefits to traditional villagers. Their water is cleaner. Their health improves. They've learned about crop rotation, fertilizers, and irrigation, greatly increasing their food supply. Some of the village children receive an education. Once they are literate, they get paying jobs, bringing the first significant cash into the community. Eventually, this will lead to electrification, running water, and communication with the outside world.

The problem is in the numbers. A process like this one might increase a village's measurable wealth two- , three- , or even four-fold. But with the village population multiplying, per-person wealth might actually be going down. All these new people want the same things as their parents and siblings. They leap at opportunities for better food, more substantial shelter, and contact with the world outside. Those who receive educations tend to leave, while the ones depending on more local improvements remain stuck in an ever-more-crowded village. Though this process adds a few more people to the middle class, it also increases the proportion of poor people. This is where the Poverty

Assassin takes aim at entire communities, and even whole nations.

Citizens in developed nations like our own should feel an obligation to change this. We have riches, know-how, and resources that should be enough to ensure a comfortable existence to all of the world's poor. However, we haven't even been able to take care of our own victims of the Poverty Assassin. Here in America, tens of millions of our own citizens can't share in our country's affluence. Chapter 3's Serena was one of these. She found a way to escape the Poverty Assassin's death grip. Serena managed to rise above a childhood choked by need. At a moment when she should've been looking forward to the normal challenges of adult life, she was faced with the problem of shelter. In her own life, Serena found creative ways to attack and defeat the Poverty Assassin. She then provided opportunities for others to do the same. With a million more like her, we might solve the problem throughout America. With a hundred million more we could solve it throughout the world.

ADOLESCENT REPRODUCTION

We have all heard about the problems of children raising children. We see it every time a young, unmarried girl gets pregnant. Too young for marriage, and not yet mature enough to see her problems clearly, the girl is likely to drop out of school, fail to find work, and become a greater burden to those around her. Idleness and low self-esteem leave her open to temptation. Many young, poor women fall victim to the lure of drugs while pregnant with their firstborn. That only compounds the problem, physically, emotionally, and financially. When the baby arrives, that adds another helpless mouth to feed.

When a thirteen-year-old girl gives birth, it's likely that the work of raising the infant will fall on the young mom's mother, grandmother, or some other more experienced parental figure. Far too often, this substitute parent went through the same thing herself. This is a problem that tends to repeat itself in subsequent generations.

The teen mother is likely to remain poor, and have more babies. She doesn't plan to do this. She's simply another teenager, often addicted to drugs, who is following what seem to be the dictates of her developing body. Boys want sex, so does she, so she finds plenty of prospective fathers. Her partners aren't likely to be much older than she is, and can hardly be counted on to become successful fathers. Even if a boy wants to do the right thing, and take responsibility, doing so seldom solves the problem. In almost every case he's simply not ready. Boys and girls in their teens should delay parenthood. For them, the birth of a child almost always makes troubled lives worse.

Denise grew up in this kind of family. Thirty-five years ago, when Denise's grandma was a nine-year-old girl, her family moved from a farm into the city. Her grandma had only a year of schooling, and when she enrolled in a city school, she quickly fell hopelessly behind. By the time Denise's grandma was fourteen, she was skipping school every day. She soon had an older boyfriend and got pregnant before she was fifteen. That's when her boyfriend disappeared.

Denise's grandma found new boyfriends, and by the time she was twenty, she'd had two daughters and two sons, each by a different father. She was also addicted to heroin. Her parents had thrown her out of the house, then relented, and let her back in. Denise's great-grandma took care of the babies and tried to teach her wayward daughter parenting skills. The most stable time Denise's mom can recall was when her addicted mother went to jail for a year. That's when Denise's mom stayed with a foster family, attended school regularly, and learned to read, write, keep house, and look after herself. Then Denise's grandma came home from prison, and they moved again.

When Denise's grandma turned thirty, she kicked the heroin habit and started going to the nearby church. Religion and a couple of health scares turned her around. But by this time her oldest daughter (Denise's mom) was fifteen and had her own problems. She'd followed in her mother's footsteps, acquiring a drug dealer boyfriend, a taste for crack cocaine, and her own teenage pregnancy. Denise's grandma and great-grandparents urged her mom to dump the boyfriend, stop smoking crack, and move back home. She did dump her boyfriend, but instead of moving home, she started dealing crack, which paid for a nice apartment.

The apartment lasted two months. When Denise was born, her mom had complications and was laid up in bed for weeks. When she finally got better, she found she'd lost most of her drug clientele. Over the next dozen years, Denise's mom bounced between addiction and recovery, had a second daughter, and moved through a series of increasingly shabby apartments.

This was Denise's world. She grew up on the streets, attending school only when the authorities forced her to. When Denise turned thirteen, she could read a little, do simple arithmetic, and she'd had her first experience with crack. When she was ready to buy some, she went to a boy named Webb. Webb supplied her for the next month and got her pregnant.

By this time, Denise's mom was in jail in another state and wasn't even aware that she would soon be a grandmother. Denise's forty-four-year-old grandma heard that she would soon be a great-grandma, and began looking for her granddaughter. She knew what the young girl must be going through, and wanted to help her as much as possible. When Denise heard her grandma was looking for her, she went to see her. She found out her grandmother was married to a retired minister. The couple lived in a small, but clean, house.

Her grandma opened the door, took the poor girl in her arms, and said: "You're home."

That evening over dinner, Denise said to these two grown-ups: "I've stopped taking drugs, and I think I can stay away from them, but what else can I do? I'll need to support myself and my child, but I'm not even in high school yet. I can only read a little. Everybody tells me I'm too young to work legally. There have to be ways I can make some money without selling drugs, or my body."

The retired minister flinched: "What a terrible thought for a young mother-to-be! No one's going to let you fall so low that you would feel you had to prostitute yourself. There's never a good enough reason to do that."

Her grandma agreed. "You can't sell drugs either . . . at least not if you want to live here. If you're going to stay with us, you must realize that you have to leave that life behind—all of it."

"I know," said Denise.

"Our neighbor, Mrs. Rawlins, has been saying she needs someone to help her clean the church," said the minister. "I'm retired, but I think the new minister would hire you. It's only part-time, but you and your child can live here, and we can help you with the baby. That way, you'll have enough time to go back to school."

"I never liked school much," said Denise.

"That's just because you're so far behind," said her grandma. "Once you start to catch up, you'll love it there."

Denise moved in with them, and four months later, she had a little boy. She named him "Timothy," and everyone called him "Tim." After he was born, she returned to school, and for a year or so, things went well. Her reading and math skills improved, and she got along with her teachers. The only problem was her friends. She was drawn to misfits, gang members, and, of course, drug users. But within that crowd, she seemed to exert a positive influence.

Then she got pregnant again. At first, she said the father was a boy from school, but her friends knew she'd been dating a local drug dealer. Denise's schoolwork went downhill, and for the first time since her return, she failed a test. Soon she failed another, and the marks on her report card plummeted. She began cutting school and spending her days on the streets. She soon had a second child, and named her "Debra." When Debra was two months old, a doctor noticed needle tracks in both of Denise's arms. When the doctor asked Denise to take a blood test, she grabbed her baby girl and fled.

The following day she left for school but never returned. Her grandma and the retired minister searched everywhere, informing the police and the school authorities. They talked to her classmates and kids in the neighborhood. All they could learn was that Denise had been talking about going to New York with her drug dealer boyfriend. They talked to the boyfriend's mother, but she hadn't seen her son in months. After that, the trail went cold.

Now, this aging couple has been left with two children to raise. They are willing and able, but with two extra mouths to feed, and no additional income, they find themselves on the brink of financial hardship. However, they also have great faith, and despite all that's happened, they are optimistic. With these qualities and the mission of raising two children, they intend to break this cycle. Their love, devotion, and honesty give them a better-than-even chance of defeating the Poverty Assassin.

This is an example of the Poverty Assassin's generational strategy. He finds a family in upheaval, identifies the weakest members, and uses drugs, alcohol, gambling, or some other personal weakness to drag down each individual. Many will succumb to this assault, but some will not. What's needed is a strong belief in one's self, and in something bigger than us.

To break this generational cycle, we must better educate our children. Along with information, we must give them hope. When a young girl gets pregnant, we must give her a place to turn. That place will have to offer real hope, along with solutions. If there are stable family members who would be willing to help, they must be identified and located. If a young teen mother is willing to let others adopt her child, we should help her find families who will. The schools with the most teen pregnancies should develop more and better support programs, including quality education about reproduction, up-to-date courses in parenting skills, and daycare for student offspring. The best thing we can do is stop the problem before it starts. Young people must learn that youth is a time for learning. They must fully prepare for parenthood before allowing themselves to become parents.

UNDERNOURISHMENT CRISIS

The three things most closely associated with poverty are the items we need most for survival and a modicum of comfort: shelter, clothing, and food. We live in a society where poor people can usually get enough clothing for survival. What they find among the castoffs from others might be frayed, torn, and ill-fitting, but it's there for anyone who looks for it. Finding shelter is more difficult, but there are places, both public and private, where destitute people can come in from the elements, and find a bit of warmth in winter, or a cooling breath of air in a summer heat wave. This isn't meant to downplay the sometimes fatal effects of exposure to the elements, but solutions to these problems are within reach. When it comes to food, this isn't as obvious. America's poor still go hungry. An empty stomach is poverty's signature nightmare.

Here in a nation that's the world's biggest food exporter, many of us can't imagine that any Americans still suffer from malnutrition. In truth, it's a national scandal. This problem isn't limited to the homeless ones lining up at soup kitchens. Hunger affects anyone who has bare kitchen shelves, an empty stomach, and no money for groceries. Most of these people have roofs over their heads, and ample, if old, clothing hanging up in their closets. Many are elderly, and on fixed incomes, and many more are children dependent on adults who are needy themselves.

Some poor people truly must make choices between food and rent, or food and medicine, or food and car payments. A single mother with three small toddlers looks at her minimum wage paycheck and must decide what's more important: rent for their tiny apartment or food for their shrinking stomachs. She may also have to factor in some over-the-counter medications for her two children who have the flu. When she finally goes to the supermarket, she gets to choose from an array of food options far broader than any in the previous history. She walks into a store packed with aisle after aisle of creative products, each with its own qualities and pitfalls. To spend her meager budget effectively requires experience, research, and thought. She needs to make choices that will provide her and her family the nutrition they need to function and grow in a healthy manner.

In the course of the last century, the U.S. has led the world in the accuracy of the packaging information we put on food items. Despite this, many Americans, both rich and poor, have no idea what nutrition they need, or what they're getting. We all glance at the figures on the side of the package, but most of us know little about their meaning. We base most of our food purchases on taste, price, and whatever we feel a craving for at that moment. Parents with children are usually a little more conscientious, but most poor parents haven't been educated about how to make the best choices with their limited grocery dollars.

Those who come from affluence usually know a little about nutrition. We learn about food from school and the media. Many Americans get more food information from their habit of constant dieting than from any other source. One irony in the field of nutrition is the fact that citizens of the best-fed nation in the world find out the most about food's qualities only when we need to go without it. It's only when we reduce the amount of food we eat that we're forced to examine that food's nutrients. Dieters learn to look at protein, carbs, fat, and vitamins, as well as overall calorie counts. They're not just counting calories. They're making every calorie count.

The poor should be doing something like this. With limited funds, impoverished consumers have a greater need to get the most out of every penny. But most of the Poverty Assassin's targets are hindered by illiteracy or a lack of basic knowledge about how nutrition works. Functional illiteracy is seven times higher among the poor than in the rest of the population. Poor people are less likely to go to doctors. When they do, it's usually for emergencies, where overall nutrition takes a backseat to concerns of the particular moment. Children in poverty tend to go to overpopulated, understaffed schools. Their teachers often must spend far too much time on order, discipline, and other basics, leaving them with little time to cover matters like health and well-being.

Most schools already have programs providing needy students with free, or reduced-price lunches. Some schools also have supplementary breakfast programs that work the same way. If a free school meal program were to incorporate healthy foods with nutritional education, that could go a long way toward solving this problem. The U.S. Department of Agriculture sponsors several food education programs, including ones aimed at kids, but these voluntary programs are limited. The USDA encourages educators to take advantage of these programs, but many teachers can't find the time to make use of them.

In addition, schools in impoverished areas often take whatever local suppliers provide for their cafeterias. Though federal and state governments create guidelines and set standards, a school's budget is the final reality. If a contractor provides "junk" lunches for less money, school officials often have no choice. That means many poor kids receive school lunches—their one guaranteed meal—loaded with sugar and salt, but lacking in nutrients. These lunches look just like the meals from a thousand fast-food places—cardboard burgers, overcooked fries, and other foods of questionable origin and effect. That's why fast-food chains and markets stocked with junk-food items thrive in poor neighborhoods. This is what they got at school.

Worldwide the problem is far worse. Nearly a billion people live in a constant state of hunger. The food they get is never enough. Each year over three million children under the age of five die of malnutrition. Those who survive are often permanently stunted in their physical and mental development. Around the globe, hunger kills more people every year than AIDS, malaria, and tuberculosis combined.

The most astonishing thing about this problem is that it could be prevented. Our earth is capable of producing enough food—and it does. According to Eric Holt Gimenez, Executive Director of the Food First program at the Institute for Food and Development Policy, "Hunger is caused by poverty and inequality, not scarcity." Most experts believe the Earth's farms can support nearly ten billion people, three billion more than the current population. Not only that, these farmers are already producing that much food, but almost a third of it goes to waste.

To see the U.S. version of this problem, you might simply look at Crystal and her family. Crystal grew up with her single mom and six siblings. Her mom began shopping for groceries at the age of fifteen when Crystal was a newborn baby. Crystal's mom knew enough to explore the baby food aisle, but she had no idea what to look for. No one had trained her for this. She tried to figure out food labels, but they made no sense to her. As her first baby grew, and more came along, she gradually gravitated to junk foods. She hated cooking, and with more and more kids, when was there ever time? As a result, Crystal grew up on a steady diet of chips, soft drinks, and happy meals.

Until Crystal reached her mid-teens, she could live on this stuff. She had plenty of energy, and, unlike her mom, she didn't get fat, but her diet deficiencies did hurt her brain's development. Crystal isn't slow or disabled, but she does have difficulty focusing, and, though she can read, she can't process her reading material as well as she should.

Now Crystal is twenty. She barely managed to graduate from high school, and then got a part-time job as an assistant counselor-in-training in a youth program at her neighborhood's community center. Last year she got pregnant by her boyfriend, Harold, who works construction. They got married, and now she has a six-month-old son and another child on the way.

Crystal, Harold, and their children are taking the first step out of poverty. Though they still get food stamps, they haven't signed up for any other government benefits. But in the supermarket, Crystal hasn't progressed much further than her mom did. She stands in the aisle, reading the ingredients on packages, and wondering what it all means. She's hazy about vitamins, protein, and what an "RDA" is. She knows the packaging is supposed to tell the truth, so when she sees things like: "Provides three essential vitamins," or "heart-healthy," those seem clear enough, so she believes them.

Like many financially challenged American grocery buyers, Crystal just needs some targeted education. A few days of studying basic nutrition would tell her what she wants to know. If she ate right, she could take in all the information, and process it, even more quickly. If she'd eaten right all her life, she could be writing books about it.

As Crystal and Harold try to rise up from their impoverished backgrounds, their daily diet hurts their efforts. Their steady consumption of fast food, soda, and other empty calories carries over to their children, extending the problem into yet another generation. With impaired brains and less-than-healthy bodies, these children will grow up, always at greater risk for falling back into the clutches of the Poverty Assassin. The Poverty Assassin doesn't even have to do anything. It's like standing beneath a tree of overripe fruit. It will drop right into his hands.

CRIME

Every year, one out of every four American households is touched by crime. No other nation on earth has a crime rate that is higher. Crime and poverty have always been linked. The percentage of criminals and victims who live in poverty is far higher than that among middle- and upper-income groups. Why? It's in the way we live.

Criminals are made, not born. If a child grows up in an atmosphere of crime, criminal behavior seems natural. If the same child is raised to respect others, and to tell the truth, that child is likely to obey the laws of the community. The Poverty Assassin strikes the vulnerable first, so children are his earliest victims. One of his most lethal weapons is "crime." After all, if you have nothing, the urge just to reach out and take something strengthens.

Darnell grew up in a neighborhood riddled with crime. He was the fifth child of nine born to a mother who never saw all of her children in one place. She was addicted to crack and followed any man who could get her the drug she craved. As her children arrived, she did her best to take care of them, but she didn't know how. One-by-one she put them up with relatives and friends until she finally had to start signing them over to become wards of the state.

Darnell lived with his mom until he turned three. One day he toddled into their kitchen and found his mom passed out on the floor. Not knowing what to do, he went out into the building's hallway and started to cry. It took twenty minutes before the other tenants paid him any attention. Finally, a woman came out from her apartment and asked him what was wrong. When he led this neighbor to his mother, the neighbor called for an ambulance. His mother's recovery was slow, and the authorities stepped in. After that, Darnell and his older siblings began drifting through a variety of foster homes. In each one, Darnell managed to get into some kind of trouble. Already he was learning the ways of crime.

By the time Darnell turned eight he was starting to skip school. Soon he was running drugs for neighborhood dealers, and by the time he was eleven he'd participated in his first mugging. At fourteen he spent a year in juvenile detention, and by the time he was eighteen he'd run up a police record that would automatically guarantee him a long sentence on his first adult conviction.

Darnell had nothing. Though he'd found his long lost mom, she was still smoking crack and lived with several other crack addicts in an abandoned row house. He'd stayed there for a few days after his last stint in juvie. When he left, all he took with him was a newfound taste for drugs. He liked the way they made him feel, and he thought they also might be a way to make a living. Dealing had its downsides, but these risks seemed fairly tame compared to the chances one took when robbing people at gunpoint.

Darnell had some success dealing drugs, and it lasted about a year. By that time he controlled all the action on two street corners, and in the crack house where his dealers and runners lived. Two prostitutes, who were also customers, came to him, asking if he could do something about their abusive pimp. Darnell knew the man had friends, so he figured whatever he did to him would have to send a message. Giving the man every chance at avoiding this, Darnell found him in a bar and offered a new deal. If the pimp stopped abusing his women, Darnell would see to it that the pimp could control—and profit from—their crack habits. When the pimp turned him down, Darnell acted with swift finality. No one ever knew what had happened to the pimp, but there was no mistake about who'd taken over his business. Now Darnell was a pimp.

In the movies, Darnell would most likely rise to crime-lord status, and die in a hail of gunfire. In real life, a far more powerful rival set him up. One day, when Darnell was visiting one of his prostitutes, the police raided the house. They found drugs, evidence of prostitution, and a dozen stolen weapons. When they found Darnell hiding in a closet, he came out swinging. He assaulted two policemen before they subdued him. One of the policemen spent a week in the hospital. Darnell's budding crime career ended with a ten-year prison sentence.

Darnell's story is typical. Though he must be held accountable for his actions, many of his choices were dictated by the workings of the Poverty Assassin. Crime is one of the assassin's most potent weapons. Most small-time criminals are born and raised in poverty. Most drop out of school, and get caught up in the criminal justice system while they are still in their teens—some even earlier.

Darnell had a younger brother he never knew, Wendell. Born of a different father, Wendell came along about three years after Darnell's discovery of their unconscious mom. When Wendell was born, their mom was facing a three-month jail term. She went in, thinking she could get her new baby back in ninety days, but the authorities put Wendell in their foster care system.

Like his half brother, Wendell bounced from one foster family to another. But when he was nine, he managed to impress one set of parents and stay in one place for a few years. He got some quality education, and by the time he was fourteen he could read, and do math at the level of a senior in high school. Now and then Wendell got into trouble, some of it serious. At fifteen, he and two other boys broke into an office at school and took $600 in cash.

Before trial, Wendell was assigned a parole officer. When the officer read Wendell's record, he noticed the mother's name. He knew this woman and knew the fate of one of her other, older children: Darnell. At this point, Darnell was serving the second year of his ten-year sentence. The officer arranged a visit between these two young men. He took Wendell to the prison, saying it was just a field trip to show Wendell where criminals wound up. When they got there, they were questioned, frisked, then allowed into the crowded visiting room. They spoke to Darnell through a screen. These two half brothers talked to each other without knowing they were related.

"Don't do what I did," Darnell told Wendell. "It really wasn't much fun, and now I'm stuck here till I'm thirty."

"No parole?" Wendell asked.

"No way, man. I took the ten without parole 'cuz otherwise I would have to take twenty-five. They don't much like it when you beat up cops."

Only after they left did Wendell learn that he'd been talking to his half brother. "Jeez," he muttered, "my brother . . . that could be me."

"Yes, it could," said his parole officer.

When his case came up in court, Wendell told the judge about his visit with his brother. "I didn't even know who I was talking to," he said, "but still I looked at him, and knew this would be where I'd wind up if that's where you decide to put me. I know I deserve it, but whether you put me there or not, when I'm free again, I'll be doing things much, much differently. I'm sorry, and I also want to confess that I'm scared. I want to do the right thing. Whatever happens, I will." The judge let Wendell go free but put him on probation for three years. The judge also ruled that the young man's record would be expunged if he stayed out of trouble. Wendell not only stayed out of trouble; he became a model student and president of his class. He went to college on a full scholarship.

Wendell beat the odds; Darnell didn't. Wendell found a home in a family just a step above poverty. However, his foster parents believed in his potential. No one ever believed in Darnell, leaving him wide open to all of the onslaughts of the Poverty Assassin. Once an impoverished young person of color is arrested for a crime, he or she is far more likely to remain in poverty for the foreseeable future. Already lacking in education, health, and nutrition, the young convict is faced by an even bigger barrier: his criminal record. Can he overcome this? Yes. But if he's going to have the slightest chance of doing this, he must first escape the stifling grip of the Poverty Assassin. A whole generation of our youth is trying to do this.

EDUCATION

Every day most of the world's seven billion people communicate, using millions of words in hundreds of different languages. Though most of this communication is spoken, we convey and preserve many of our most vital ideas by our use of the written word. We also communicate with numbers. We use these to measure, compare, estimate, and calculate. We talk about numbers, but when we work with them, we begin by writing them on paper or putting them on a screen with our keystrokes. The practices of writing, reading, and performing mathematical functions are collectively known as "literacy." Those of us who can do these things are "literate." Those who can't are described as "illiterate."

In 2003 a U.S. government study showed that between 21% to 23% of adult Americans couldn't locate information in sections of text, make logical sense out of printed words, or easily connect identifiable ideas and descriptions printed on a page. Among those adults who rank lowest on the literacy scale, 44% live in poverty. That's more than double the national average. An estimated 130 million of the world's fifteen- to twenty-four- year-olds (about 12%) can't read or write. Though some of these illiterate young people can do the most basic arithmetic in their heads, they can't read or write numbers, which greatly limits their potential in the workplace. This ignorance is one of the Poverty Assassin's most powerful weapons. The less people can communicate, the less they learn. The less they learn, the less they can accomplish.

Reading, writing, and basic math skills are essential for a lot more than day-to-day communications. Writing allows us to store information until we need it, while reading gives us the means to retrieve data. Math provides us with functions and measurements of anything that can be quantified. With math, we can understand proportions and ratios, which help us evaluate risk and potential gains. Using all these skills together, we can examine and analyze problems, and find ways to solve them. Without these skills, we would be lost.

To see the value of literacy, let's look at two students starting high school. Jasmine and Jeff both come from families that have suffered at the hands of the Poverty Assassin. Their hardworking parents are poor, mostly due to a lack of education. However, Jasmine's mother reads and enjoys doing it. She's passed her fondness for books on to her daughter. Jasmine reads well, gets good marks, and hopes to win a scholarship to college. Jeff doesn't have this advantage. His parents can barely read at all. They would like to see Jeff do better in school, but they don't know how to help him. Jeff can read and write his name, and recognizes some words. He can't read instructions, warnings, or news stories. He's reached high school simply because he's stayed out of trouble and received social promotions each year. He attends a high school where this is a common practice.

In her first year of high school, Jasmine excels, doing well in every subject. In addition to her textbooks, she also reads magazines, websites, novels, and books about current events. When she learns something new, she can analyze it, and fit it into her existing knowledge.

Jasmine's teachers take notice of this high-achieving student. Her math teacher helps Jasmine get a part-time job as a clerk in a women's clothing store. Though she tends to be shy with customers, her boss, Mrs. Brown, notices that Jasmine has a head for figures. Mrs. Brown starts teaching Jasmine some of the basics of the business, starting with the daily receipts. Once Jasmine has learned the store's accounting system, she begins suggesting improvements. She creates a new, more efficient inventory program, and talks to the store's accountant about taxes, payroll, and overhead expenses. By the time Jasmine graduates from high school, Mrs. Brown has decided to help this young lady with college expenses. She urges Jasmine to go to a local university. That way, Jasmine can keep working at the store.

Jeff is not so fortunate. He soon finds that his high school teachers aren't going to promote him automatically, the way his grade school did. By the end of Jeff's first semester, his student counselor, Mr. Miller, warns him that being held back a year is a definite possibility. Mr. Miller recommends remedial reading and math classes. Jeff attends these for a few sessions, but when he can't keep up, he quits. By the time he's sixteen, Jeff has dropped out of high school, and begun taking drugs. He develops an addiction to crack that costs a few hundred dollars a week. To cover this expense, he starts dealing crack, but his negligible math skills defeat his efforts, and he soon finds himself deeply in debt to some very dangerous people. One of

Jeff's customers, Brian, suggests that Jeff help him stick up a store.

"I don't know," Jeff says. "I've never even fired a gun."

"You won't have to," Brian tells him. "I'll be the one with the gun. You're my driver."

Though the robbery goes off without a hitch, someone sees the getaway, recognizing the car, and taking down the license number. Ten minutes later, the police find both young men in an alley, where Brian is showing Jeff how to change the car's license plates.

When the police interrogate them separately, Brian talks first, blaming everything on Jeff. He quickly negotiates a plea deal and agrees to testify against his accomplice. Jeff's interrogators show him the printout of Brian's statement and keep referring to it in their questioning. Too embarrassed to admit his illiteracy, Jeff stares at the document, but he also listens attentively to his interrogators. He assumes he'll learn what's in the document from their questions. This doesn't work. By the time he figures out that Brian has turned on him, Jeff has already said far too much. Brian gets a suspended sentence, while Jeff goes to prison for five years.

These teenagers' stories are typical. Basic reading and math skills change lives, and usually for the better. They are essential components in the language of success. Illiteracy and ignorance are among the Poverty Assassin's most powerful weapons. Real literacy is a vital component in any long-term effort to eradicate poverty. Teenagers and adults should be able to read and write. They must learn enough about the words they use to understand basic analysis. They must understand the words, and how they connect and convey thoughts and ideas.

In our efforts to solve the problems in our schools and on our streets, literacy and learning are our most powerful weapons. If a child can read well, a whole world opens, full of potential and opportunity. Illiteracy often leads to despair, addiction, and even life behind bars. Whether parents are literate or not, they should do everything they can to encourage their children's reading. One of the most positive steps an illiterate parent can take is to admit the problem and sign up for an adult education course in reading. Most localities have free programs that provide this service.

HEALTHCARE

A recent Gallup Poll revealed that, despite the passage of the Affordable Care Act in 2011, 13.4% of Americans say they still don't have health insurance. Most of these people are working poor—those who get a regular paycheck, but no employee health benefits. Their hourly pay is usually under $15 per hour. Once they've paid for food, shelter, clothing, and transportation, they have very little left for health insurance. Though many of these people could qualify for partial government subsidies, they still have to pay their part, and that's often beyond their means.

The United States spends more on healthcare than any other country. This is true whether you measure total dollars, or per person. For all that money, we come in thirty-eighth in life expectancy at age sixty among the nations of the world. Some of the nations that do better in this key area aren't that surprising. That Japan, and most eurozone nations, are ahead of us might be troubling, but it's understandable. They are developed (and thus affluent) nations, just like us. That we pay twice as much as they do for our slightly inferior healthcare is not understandable, or even acceptable, yet it's true. Compared to others, we don't get much for our healthcare dollars.

Then there are countries like Chile, Cambodia, Venezuela, Suriname, and several others. These impoverished nations pay their healthcare providers a small fraction of what we pay ours, yet they get a better product. This doesn't bother America's rich, or those middle-class earners whose employers provide so-called "Cadillac plans." They get the best care money can buy. The Americans who suffer from this disparity are the poor. In most other countries, the poor have access to basic healthcare services. Here our healthcare system provides the Poverty Assassin with some of his best tools: stress, procrastination, inattention, and apathy.

Americans tend to think of healthcare in terms of costs, insurance, and co-pays, but the complete picture is more complex. Healthcare begins with people. When we're sick, we want to get well. When we're very sick, or badly hurt, we want to see a doctor. When we're covered by insurance, we can. When we're not, this gets more difficult.

Kendra is a thirty-three-year-old single mother of two. She graduated from high school, started community college, but only got a dozen credits before she dropped out to get married. Her husband disappeared after the birth of their second child. She now manages a convenience store and makes $13 per hour. Her compensation doesn't include health coverage. Kendra has insured her ten-year-old, Barry, and her eight-year-old, Sonia, through a state-funded program available through their public school. When she looked into subsidized insurance for herself, she learned that she would have to pay $125 per month out-of-pocket or $1,500 per year. Though she knew that her tax refund would be nearly wiped out by penalties at tax time, she went without the insurance. Then her knees began to hurt.

After weeks of hobbling around, Kendra woke up one morning, unable to walk. Her son, Barry, found a neighbor who lent her crutches, but whenever she moved about, her pain was still excruciating. Finally, she called a physician a friend had recommended: Dr. Harvey.

Over the phone, Dr. Harvey's receptionist asked Kendra several questions. One was about insurance. As soon as Kendra said that she wasn't insured, the tone of the conversation changed.

"Dr. Harvey doesn't have any openings right now, or in the near future," said the receptionist. "Perhaps, you'd do better with someone else."

"Do you have any recommendations?" Kendra asked, wincing from the throb in her left knee.

The receptionist gave her a name.

When Kendra called the second doctor, she had an almost identical conversation with another receptionist. Again she hung up with nothing but another doctor's name and number. This happened five times in a row. When the fifth receptionist unknowingly referred her back to Dr. Harvey, Kendra cried: "He was the first one I called!"

"I'm sorry," said the receptionist. "We're quite busy this time of year. The next opening isn't likely to be anytime soon. Perhaps you should go to the ER. Though you might have to wait for a while, they have to treat you. It's the law."

Kendra took this advice. Still, in great pain, she waited four hours. Finally, she saw a physician's assistant who said she probably had rheumatoid arthritis. He gave her a shot and told her it was a long-term condition that would need constant attention. She spent her last $20 on a prescription and went home. Within a couple of hours, the pain subsided. The next day she was back at work. When she asked the store owner, Mr. Lane, about the possibility of a health insurance policy, he said: "I'm almost going broke as it is."

Three weeks later, her knee pain flared up again. Kendra took more pills, but they barely put a dent in her suffering. She called in sick each morning. When she failed to call in on the fourth morning (she overslept), Mr. Lane fired her. Without her paycheck, she would soon qualify for Medicaid, but if she found another low-paying job, any Medicaid benefits would either be reduced or gone.

If Kendra were to have her usual income and a good insurance package, she would be able to afford to go back to school. She'd always wanted to study to become a dental technician, but tuition was just out of reach. Every day she wondered how life itself could be so expensive.

Kendra's desperation is common. Disease, injury, and chronic conditions are three of the Poverty Assassin's favorite tools in the quest to keep poor people poor. In theory, healthcare is now available to everyone in the United States. However, the theory doesn't always work out in practice. If your financial picture is good, you almost certainly have good health insurance, making everything easier. When you get sick, you call the doctor. When you need a prescription, you go to the drugstore. Many insurers have reduced their customer's paperwork to a minimum. Many doctors bill the insurer directly, only asking patients for payment if it only amounts to a small co-pay.

For the poor, it's a different story. Someone like Kendra must navigate through the confusing seas of bureaucracy. Though she can always get healthcare, nothing is automatic. She has to answer questions, fill out forms, and make choices between bad and worse options. If she decides to pay for private insurance, she will probably have to accept a policy with a deductible of several thousand dollars. In most years, such a policy won't pay for much of anything.

In the last few decades, America's poor have learned again and again that their healthcare choices are severely limited. They've seen friends and relatives lose their life savings to diseases that have ravaged their bodies. They watched as promising young lives were permanently limited by mountains of debt. These experiences have made the poor suspicious of all medical professionals. As a result, many poor people stay away from all healthcare professionals until it's too late. They wind up in ambulances and clogged emergency rooms, seeking treatment for problems that should have been simple, but are now life-threatening.

The Affordable Care Act grew from the best of intentions. It's increased the number of people who have health insurance by several million. (Different sources give different numbers, but all agree that more people are now insured.) But there's a coverage gap affecting the working poor. According to the Kaiser Foundation, about four million people fall into this gap. Over ten times that many — an estimated forty-one million individuals — were still without health coverage in 2013. Until the world's richest nation finds a way to solve this problem, healthcare will continue to give the Poverty Assassin an unending supply of victims.

BUSINESS DEVELOPMENT

In the past few years business has gotten a bad rap. Some of this is earned; some isn't. The economic meltdown of 2008 and the subsequent hard times left many people homeless and jobless. The poor have been particularly hard hit. During the meltdown, the most public face of business was that of the banks. Much of the blame they got was well-deserved. But not all businesses are banks.

The biggest business transaction most people ever make is buying a home. The real estate bubble of the early 2000s dangled the dream of homeownership in front of millions of "working" poor families. When the bubble burst, the Poverty Assassin had these families in its sights, and mowed them down en masse, littering the landscape with foreclosures. Though many individual home buyers blamed their Realtors, most Americans felt the prime culprits were the banks. These financial institutions had lent far too much money, with too little collateral. When enough home buyers fell behind in their payments, bankers began to panic. A panicky banker almost always does the same thing: demand payment. This makes the banker the active agent of the Poverty Assassin.

Businesses should be good for a community. A street lined with thriving businesses usually means jobs, paychecks, and more options for local consumers. Successful businesses that give back to their communities are fundamental building blocks for a successful neighborhood. A business that's a good corporate citizen works with its community to solve problems, create jobs, and encourage education.

Many impoverished neighborhoods have few locally owned businesses, and too many chain stores and franchises owned by outsiders. While some of these outsider-owned businesses take an interest in their neighborhoods, too many don't. Some of these stores and services suck money out of their community and give back nothing. Others provide employment, participate in training programs, and furnish healthcare, pensions, and other benefits.

Juan's twelve-square-block neighborhood of one thousand homes and apartments is anchored by an aging shopping center. We'll call the neighborhood "Westerly." The shopping center, Westerly Commons, occupies one full square block on the neighborhood's north end. With one entrance just off the nearby expressway, middle- and high-income customers from the suburbs can visit the stores without ever having to drive through any part of Westerly.

A few years ago, Westerly also had two churches and an elementary school. Up until just a few years ago, ten mom-and-pop storefronts dotted the neighborhood's streets. Two corner groceries, one drugstore, and a small hardware store had all been open for over two decades. In addition, there were two thrift stores, a barbershop, two gas stations, and a beauty salon.

Westerly Commons has been there since the '70s. It went through a major renovation about ten years ago, at the height of the real estate boom. At that time there was a lot of talk of targeting Westerly for re-gentrification. Though the talk was just rumored, and no clear plans emerged, local Realtors began selling homes to working-poor buyers. The Realtors enticed them with easy terms, no down payments, and visions of huge profits when they moved.

Two banks with branches in Westerly Commons provided most of the neighborhood's mortgages. Their strategy was simple but flawed. They would put industrious working-poor families in these houses. These thrifty homeowners would keep the structures from deteriorating further, and attend to some basic cosmetics like painting and sidewalk repair. Once the neighborhood began looking a little better, the banks would start marketing these homes to upscale buyers, who would then make the major renovations suitable to their much higher incomes. The bankers and Realtors would make money when the working poor bought, and even more when they sold. In between they would loan money to the "working" poor owners for basic home improvements. If the strategy worked, everyone would be happy. If it didn't—that was something the bankers didn't seem to consider.

Then the bubble burst. Juan had grown up in Westerly. He'd gone to school here, and found his first job here, as an apprentice to a neighborhood carpenter. Soon Juan was a carpenter himself, working on construction sites. In 2006 he bought a three-bedroom row house for $35,000. A few months after that, a similar house down the street went for $50,000. Juan got to work. He painted, put in new kitchen appliances, and sealed the basement, all for just over $14,000. He'd hoped to sell his house for as much as $80,000 in the coming years. Then came the downturn.

In 2009 Juan lost his job. A few months later, his savings ran out. Two months after that, he maxed out what was left of his credit. Facing foreclosure and bankruptcy, Juan told his Realtor he wanted to sell. They put the house on the market for $50,000, but quickly reduced it to $40,000. Two more reductions finally found a buyer who paid $30,000. The new owner offered to let Juan continue living there for $500 per month. Juan did this for six months, then moved out of Westerly. He wanted to go somewhere new, and have a fresh start.

Of the ten mom-and-pop businesses, only three are still open: one barbershop, the beauty salon, and the drugstore. The one big-box store in Westerly Commons survived, but among its forty other storefront businesses, only eighteen held on. Over half closed. Most of the closings were locally owned shops. The bank branches are still there, as are most of the chain store franchises.

The neighborhood's homeowners were badly hit. In the five years leading up to the meltdown, there'd been four hundred home sales—about eighty per year. Among the homeowners who had stayed put, just over half had refinanced their mortgages. The average price of these little row houses had jumped from $23,000 to $44,000, and everyone thought (and hoped) they would just keep rising. That dream quickly faded with the recession. By the time Juan moved, a third of Westerly's homes had gone into foreclosure. Over a hundred houses had been deserted, and many of these were boarded up. Houses that had been split into apartments did better. Some evicted homeowners moved into the apartments, and only five of these houses went into foreclosure. However, landlords have had to lower rents, and they are getting behind on repairs. Westerly's elementary school has closed, sending its students to a larger school a mile away. Even one of the churches shut their doors.

Juan left Westerly, feeling as if he'd been defeated. He found an inexpensive apartment in another part of town, and in 2011 he got a job with a local contractor specializing in home renovation. When Juan suggested that the contractor look at homes in Juan's old neighborhood, the contractor wound up buying three of them. At Juan's urging, the contractor then hired several young people in the neighborhood, and Juan formed them into a crew. They gutted the houses, then renovated them, putting in only the most basic features. With moderately priced materials, they made these old houses into reasonably comfortable, newly refurbished homes. The contractor then sold these homes to working people who had enough income to meet the reasonable mortgage payments. This started a trend. Two other contractors followed. Soon Westerly was being repopulated by lower-income working families, avoiding the dislocation of re-gentrification. This past year, Juan bought a home and moved back to the neighborhood where he feels that he belongs. Next year he has plans to open his own hardware store. His current boss and two other local business owners are backing him.

As The Poverty Assassin knows, neighborhoods like Westerly are a lot like organisms. When the neighborhood is healthy, all of its parts work together. Locally owned businesses provide jobs, goods, and services. They hire young people from the neighborhood, teaching them their first occupational skills. They participate in programs encouraging literacy and healthcare. Their owners reinvest in the neighborhood. In a healthy neighborhood, banks understand their role. They want property values to rise, but their primary aim isn't speedy turnover. They want to give mortgages to buyers who will move in with their families and stay. They know the value of small businesses, education, and faith-based communities. With these tools, the working poor can rise into the middle class, often without ever moving away from their roots.

The first goal of a business is profit, but not all profit is measured in dollars and cents. Though business owners must make hard decisions, they must also appreciate their communities. When a bank loans someone money for a home or business, the banker's job is to make sure the loan is profitable, secure, and good for the community. When local businesses thrive, they should give back to their communities. When banks, businesses, and homeowners work together, they thwart the Poverty Assassin. When they don't, they are handing him a potent weapon.

JOB CREATION

Jobs are the foundation of healthy families, neighborhoods, towns, and nations. Jobs are work, and any worthwhile work has meaning. Without jobs, people lose income, but even worse, they lose purpose. Working and producing is an essential part of our identity. Even when we meet someone who's retired, one of our first questions is: "What do you do?" When the answer is "nothing," we usually feel we have reason to wonder why.

Jobs are our primary defense against the assaults of the Poverty Assassin. Unemployment is the wedge he uses to get his foot in the door. When a business goes into a tailspin, the boss lays off staff. Workers go home with this news, and suddenly, whole families live in fear. This process begins with the laid-off worker. He or she fears rejection by other employers, long lines at the unemployment office, empty days of idleness, plummeting self-esteem, and the slow frittering away of benefits and life savings. Spouses fear that their own resources will fall short as their partner's crisis continues. Older children see these fears in their parents and learn about some of life's dangers for the first time. Younger children understand none of this, but they sense the concerns of their elders and fear the unknown.

If the wage earner's idleness extends over months, or even years, the effects can be extremely debilitating, sometimes leaving lifelong scars. In some instances, these idle workers and their families have to move out of their homes in more affluent neighborhoods, into smaller, less desirable houses and apartments. All too often, unemployment causes families to break apart. Parents divorce, children leave home before they're really ready, and the family home is abandoned. This can be the end of a family. When it happens throughout a working-class neighborhood like Westerly, the whole community is at risk. When a community loses its wage earners, its very soul can be threatened.

Some businesses thrive on such hardship. Unemployment means idleness. Those who have too much time on their hands will often turn to drugs or drinking. Too many bars and liquor stores can erode a neighborhood's cohesiveness. Though the unemployed have little money, often they spend what they can get in these establishments. This can lead to missed rent and mortgage payments, less money for food, health, and other necessities, increased friction within the household, and more domestic violence.

The same holds for businesses that thrive on gambling. Lotto tickets, slot machines, and other wagering vehicles lure in those for whom risk-taking grows into a disease. The addicted gambler always sees the big score just ahead, and thus always justifies the wasting of another dollar. Winning is just a chance to bet more, which brings the inevitable losses. Those who always gamble almost always lose everything. In a way that's what they are seeking. The glint in their eyes that looks so much like desperate hope is actually self-destructive masochism.

Businesses that thrive on human weakness always hold out the promise of jobs and income for their communities, but these jobs come with a huge price. When we view bars, liquor stores, and casinos, each worker's paycheck must be balanced against a jobless person's depleted bank account and unpaid bills. Each business owner's profits come at the cost of evictions, failed marriages, and worse.

Businesses that feed on misery earn the enmity of their neighbors. A bar owner who fails to give back to the community will often see his business fail, too. A neighborhood store owner who preys on gambling addictions with his lottery franchise sometimes sees the rest of his business decline. Many of these predators accept this as a part of their business model. They sign short-term leases, move in, make a killing, then close and move on.

But there are plenty of beneficial businesses, and, as we've seen in the previous chapter, those businesses need employees. One important question is: where will these workers come from? When an entrepreneur opens a small business in a neighborhood like Westerly, will that entrepreneur look to the neighborhood for employees? With some businesses, the possibilities are limited. When Mr. Jones opens a realty office, he needs salespeople with real estate licenses. Westerly doesn't have any, so Mr. Jones must look elsewhere.

However, when Ms. Miller opens a diner, she needs cooks, dishwashers, and waitstaff. Though she could advertise all over the area, the pastor of Westerly's surviving church urges her to seek out candidates from the neighborhood. The pastor tells her about Carl Bowers, a former short-order cook, who's been patching together an income from odd jobs for the past six years. When Ms. Miller offers Carl a reasonable and regular paycheck, he leaps at the opportunity.

Carl helps Ms. Miller recruit neighborhood residents for six of the other eight kitchen positions. Four of these are high-school-age part-timers. Her other two hires from Westerly will work a full week schedule. One is Army veteran, Sally Tebbs. The other, Joe Jefferson, is nearing sixty. He lost his last job three years ago, and he and his wife have been worried that he might never work again. Ms. Miller then puts together her floor staff—waitpeople and one full-time cashier—entirely from the neighborhood.

When Westerly's church hosts a meeting of neighborhood leaders and business owners, Ms. Miller and Mr. Jones meet. When Mr. Jones talks of the lack of qualified Realtors in the neighborhood, Ms. Miller asks him: "Why not offer to train someone from around here?"

"It's not that simple," he tells her. "They have to attend a class, earn a certificate, then get a license."

"So?" she counters. "When I first started working, I didn't know the first thing about diners. I got a job bussing tables, then I was a waitress, and for a while, I cooked. I had to learn my business, just like you had to learn yours. I have to train waitstaff and kitchen help, just like somebody trained me. I do it every time I hire someone new. I train them because, in the end, I profit from it. Every licensed Realtor you have makes you money, right?"

"That's true," Mr. Jones admits. "Otherwise, I wouldn't keep them on."

"So why not train one or two from right around here? They could work in your office, learning the routine, while they take the class. Once someone from Westerly has a license, that person could specialize in sales here in the neighborhood."

"But that's another problem," says Mr. Jones. "Hardly any homeowners in this neighborhood come to me to sell their houses."

Ms. Miller smiles. "If you had a Realtor who lives here, that might change."

Mr. Jones scratches his head, and says: "That's not such a bad idea."

A month later, Mr. Jones hires a middle-aged Westerly woman named Debra. She learns the office routine quickly and starts attending real estate class that spring. A year later she's handling over half the home sales in the neighborhood. From now on, whenever Westerly homeowners decide to sell, they know an honest broker who lives and works right around the corner.

There are limits to this kind of direct action. A residential neighborhood's businesses usually can't provide jobs for all of its workers, or even a majority of them. But most small businesses need workers, both full-time and part-time. Many of these positions are the types of jobs young people can fill. Eateries need kitchen and floor staff. Shops need clerks, and stores need cashiers. Every time an entrepreneur hires a teenager to fill one of these slots, it creates an opportunity to teach the value of trust, reliability, and precision. Small businesses provide a setting where young people can see how free enterprise works. One day some of them will start their own businesses. When they do, they'll have many of the skills they need because they learned them right in the neighborhood.

These jobs can also serve as safety nets for neighborhood residents who are temporarily out of work, or families that need some additional income. A longtime stay-at-home parent might take a part-time position as a way of reentering the labor market, while someone who's exhausted his or her unemployment benefits could regard even a low-wage paycheck as a necessary lifeline. In this way, small businesses can be a part of the glue that holds a community together.

Neighborhoods must take an interest in their businesses, and businesses must invest in their neighborhoods. When both sides do this, individuals, families, and communities thrive. When they don't, neighborhoods become inviting targets for the Poverty Assassin.

COMMUNITY CAPACITY BUILDING / CAPACITY DEVELOPMENT

Chapter 12's Ms. Miller and Mr. Jones are building businesses, but they are also building something bigger: a thriving community. The same is true of Janet in Chapter 2, Serena in Chapter 3, and Juan in Chapter 11. Each one starts with a personal goal: solving a parking dilemma, finding a home off the street, or returning to the old neighborhood. Each realizes that he or she can't do it alone.

Janet's specific parking dispute is with her next-door neighbor, but the parking problem affects her neighborhood as a whole. Serena is homeless due to her personal situation, but she enters a community where no one has a home. Juan's connection with Westerly is deep, personal, and lifelong, but if he's going to get back there, he must work with others to help his old neighborhood recover from hard times. Ms. Miller and Mr. Jones start out to make a profit, but they soon discover that success in business often depends on their success as citizens of their community.

All of these people are building the capacities of their communities. In Chapter 2, Janet moves onto a street where parking is an issue. When the problem touches her, she acts constructively. If she were only concerned with herself, she would see her neighbor, Mr. Knot, as an enemy. Instead, she involves him in the parking problem in a way that invites him to put his passion for orderliness to work. She gives him the power to help solve the problem, but she also limits that power by requiring him to pay attention to other points of view.

In Chapter 3, Serena starts from a far less advantageous position. While Janet's new home is a measure of her success, Serena's lack of any home at all would seem to be an object lesson in failure. Serena refuses to see it that way. When life gives her lemons, she mixes up some lemonade. She identifies the seat of power in the person of the Boss Man, Link. She looks for work, and finds a job she can do. This leads her to find her own apartment. Once she's gotten herself off the street, she doesn't stop there. She returns to her homeless community, enlists Link's help, and they begin creating an avenue for others to rise up and out of that world.

In Chapters 11 and 12, Juan, Ms. Miller, and Mr. Jones all have an interest in Westerly. Juan wants to move back to his old neighborhood, while Ms. Miller and Mr. Jones want to build their businesses there. Each acts from self-interest, but all three must involve others. Inevitably their constructive actions help Westerly recover.

All of these stories are tales of concerned citizens building their community's capacities. Janet averts a fight with her new neighbor by empowering him to help all their neighbors. Serena parlays her need for work into an effort to get work for Link and other homeless people. This will get them off the streets, and into their own rooms and apartments. The less homeless there are, the better it is for the larger community.

"Community Capacity Building" (also referred to as "capacity development") can stop the Poverty Assassin, eject him from the lives of his victims, and keep him away. This conceptual approach focuses on identifying obstacles and bringing people together to overcome them. It applies to international organizations, governments, nongovernmental organizations (NGOs), as well as schools, churches, and neighborhoods. When you develop a community's capacity for positive action, you help its citizens reach their goals. When you begin with a specific goal (like parking, housing, or business development), you will often find yourself creating a framework for broader progress. Community members can use this framework to achieve measurable and sustainable results.

"Community capacity building" is the process of strengthening people's skills, competencies, and abilities, enabling them to overcome their isolation and suffering and connect with others. This process helps people join together in communities to solve common problems, including those of housing, hunger, education, crime, sanitation, and employment. These efforts are key factors in lifting whole communities out of poverty.

A community is any group of people who connect with one another for certain purposes and actions. Some communities are loose groupings on the Internet—gamers, bloggers, or any collection of people with similar interests. More traditional communities are identified by occupation, beliefs, jurisdictions, and geographical borders, both man-made and natural. A church is a community of people who share a set of spiritual beliefs, and faith in the same God. A professional organization is a community of people who are qualified to work in a particular field. The American Medical Association and the American Bar Association are classic examples of these. A state, or nation, is a community whose citizens are connected by a common loyalty to, and acceptance of, a particular government's authority. A national community is often also defined by accepted geographical borders, as well as societal traditions and mores.

Most of our examples have concerned neighborhoods. These have geographical borders, and often share other interests. A neighborhood might have several different churches, each representing a particular faith. Most neighborhoods have a school or two, and citizens who work at various occupations. Each citizen starts with his or her wants and needs. A citizen who goes it alone usually comes up against stifling limitations. That's when the citizen must look at his or her personal goals, and see where these coincide with the actions of the community.

Janet gets an annoying neighbor off her back by appealing to his talents and engaging him to use those talents to help others. Serena finds her way out of homelessness by creating a route others can travel to achieve the same aim. Juan uses his skills to work his way back to Westerly, then helps others in the effort to lift that neighborhood out of poverty, and into the middle class. Ms. Miller and Mr. Jones use their business acumen to create enterprises whose profits are inextricably linked to Westerly's increasing prosperity.

For most of us who live in towns and cities, our neighborhoods are our most immediate communities. They are the basic structures within which we live our lives. They give us order, peace, education, freedom from crime, healthcare, commerce, and all the other fruits of communal cooperation—the things we can't do alone. If these communities are going to have any chance of working, their members must be willing to work hard, speak their minds, and compromise with each other.

Today, we face increasingly complex social problems with limited financial resources. Most traditional institutions—government, business, and nonprofits—have to do more with less, creating a growing demand for engaging people in problem-solving. A community's capacity is that of all of its members working together. If we don't share this workload, our community will disintegrate. But if all of us can find ways to achieve our most essential goals, while helping others to achieve theirs, then our community's potential for positive development is infinite. When that happens, a community can cast the Poverty Assassin into permanent exile.

SOCIAL CONSCIOUSNESS & THE HUMAN CAPITAL SOLUTION

The Poverty Assassin kills some, wounds many, and has a chilling effect on all of us. With his most direct victims, he strangles their hopes, saps their spirits, and squeezes them, draining all ambition and energy from their lives. He stalks his prey with the threats of ignorance, joblessness, and depression. Once he has poor people in his grasp, he keeps them isolated in slum neighborhoods that are more like prisons—no one can get out, and no one on the outside wants to get in.

This killer of people and dreams crosses national borders and then does the same thing all over the world. The most impoverished nations are like poor neighborhoods but on a much larger scale. Countries like Sudan, Malawi, Haiti, and Nepal are among the Poverty Assassin's worst victims. Their schools are few and lack basic educational tools, such as paper, pencils, and books. Digital devices and systems are out of the question. Only the very richest citizens have computers, phones, or even electricity.

Their farms can't produce enough food, and they have no money to buy any from better-off nations. Their roads are poor, and vast areas have no modern transportation at all. All of these problems combine to keep these countries poor and disconnected. Those of us in the developed world have no immediate reason to visit these places. Many of their people yearn to leave, but they have no way to get out. Like the impoverished neighborhood, the chronically poor nation is almost totally forgotten and ignored. Few visit, and even fewer leave.

In some ways, the solution is complex, multifaceted, and difficult. In one way, it is simple.

We've reviewed many of the problems and complexities. Every person living in an alley, or under a highway overpass, has his or her own individual story. One might be there because he lost his job, another because she was evicted. One might be too old to work, while the other is too young for legal employment. Poor kids desperately need quality education, yet poor neighborhoods traditionally receive only the last few pennies of the state's educational dollar. In such an atmosphere, ignorance breeds ignorance, and, as we've seen, illiteracy breeds more illiteracy. Crime springs up from multiple sources. It's easy for someone who's always needy to succumb to callousness and greed. Someone who knows only despair is far more likely to find solace in drugs and/or liquor, and then develop addictions. This process concentrates street crime in the most impoverished neighborhoods, where the police struggle simply to keep some semblance of order.

All of these problems are a part of a web woven by the Poverty Assassin. Foreclosure rips people from their homes, decimating neighborhoods. Families disintegrate, and soon, child mothers are having babies long before they are ready. These children of children grow up hungry and illiterate. Their ignorance makes them unemployable. Idleness leads to depression, which is eased by drugs. Drugs require cash, which is most easily gained through crime. Crime leads to prison, and when the criminal gets out, he's released into a culture of increasing want and deprivation. The quickest way for him to earn the respect of his peers is to become a more successful criminal.

How can we deal with this insidious cycle? We must begin with the simplest quality of all: human decency. The essential tool we have is our own inner need to do the right thing. This doesn't mean that all of us have to do everything. It simply means that we must open our eyes, examine the problems right in front of us, then, after taking stock of our own individual talents and resources, we should do the tasks we are able to do. It's really that simple, and it's really that hard. Doing the right thing is usually both.

If you are an elected official, this might mean creating innovative programs, enacting legislation, and inspiring your constituents. If you are a community activist, church official, or just a concerned citizen, doing the right thing means targeting specific problems, and joining together with others to solve them. A teacher might start with a particular child or a whole classroom of children. An entrepreneur could begin by hiring and training his or her first employee.

Most victims of the Poverty Assassin aren't excused from this mission. If you live in poverty, but you're able to act, you must do so. The mother who can't read should learn how for her sake, and for that of her children. She must enter the class, concentrate on the work, and find her way into the world of the written word. If you are unemployed, you must go out and find a job. If none are available, look for whatever work you can find. Don't allow discouragement or pride to get in your way. If you can do something that earns you a few honest dollars, do it. Once you have some cash in hand, use it wisely. Don't spend it all on a restaurant meal when the same amount gets you food for several meals from the grocery store.

A homeless person who wants a home must make a real effort to find one. Examine the problem. Recognize real possibilities, and then chart a path that will take you there. Do you need a job first? Get one. Do you need a full stomach? Swallow your pride, and head for the soup kitchen. Do you need help from others? Seek it politely, but assertively. Go to churches, community centers, employment offices—anyplace where you might find assistance in creating short- and long-term solutions.

Most of us here in the U.S. aren't poor. The Poverty Assassin affects us only indirectly. Some of us might be victims of crime. The value of our homes might be threatened by nearby foreclosures and abandoned buildings. Our local public schools might be turning into nothing more than wholesale babysitters for unruly children suffering from too little protein and too much sugar. But we are all members of our local communities. Some of us live in cities, others on farms. No matter where we live, it's likely that the Poverty Assassin is working not far away.

Those of us who are "haves" are obligated by the needs of the "have-nots." Why? Because they are members of our human family. In many ways, they are the same as us. When we turn our backs on them, we are turning on ourselves as well.

If you have a whole lot of money, you can always just write a few checks to your favorite causes, but remember: it takes more than that. If you can teach reading, math, or an essential skill, then look for a place to do it. If you can build and repair things, use your skills to help others create comfortable spaces for living and working. If you've beaten an addiction, volunteer to help others follow in your footsteps. If you don't know what you can do, go to your local church, mosque, synagogue, school, hospital, or community center, and start asking what they need. If you're willing, they will find plenty of ways for you to help others.

All these efforts have a common source: human decency. It's our primary weapon when battling the Poverty Assassin. An act of human decency is an expression of the best in ourselves. When one person does a good deed, it helps all of us to be all that we can be, enabling us to help others. In other words, it "pays it forward."

The Poverty Assassin has been hard at work ever since the first person went hungry. He's been turning people out of their homes, taking food from the mouths of babies, and spreading ignorance and desolation for thousands of years. As people joined together to live in villages, towns, and cities, the Poverty Assassin saw his opportunity. What he'd always done retail, he could now do wholesale.

Though people had banded together for the protections a community can bring, the Poverty Assassin recognized the potential for distraction, division, and conflict. In these much larger groups, he used his age-old tools of greed, envy, and violence to trap his victims.

We must return to the first reasons for community. In our neighborhoods, towns, cities, and nations, we must find common ground that connects us all; then we must stand united against the Poverty Assassin. Using the tools of knowledge and communication, we must find our collective wisdom, and learn to see the best in each other. When others are in need, we must extend a helping hand. When they can begin to take steps on their own, we must light the path, and encourage them to help themselves. If we believe in ourselves, and do right by each other, the day will soon come when our community will be proud to be judged by the character of its citizens.

MASS INCARCERATION

On May 1, 2015, a crowd of nearly two thousand people marched through Baltimore's streets in a demonstration urging peace and responsibility. This mass gathering of protestors was quite calm, orderly, and unified, especially in light of the recent events in that city. Baltimore had been on edge for nearly three weeks after a twenty-five-year-old African-American male named Freddie Gray suffered fatal injuries during his arrest and transport to a Baltimore police station. Gray lingered for six days after his altercation with the police. His death sparked civil disturbances near Baltimore's Camden Yards. Two days after he died, in the hours just after his funeral, the city had erupted in the worst rioting since the violence that had followed Martin Luther King's death forty-seven years earlier.

A few hours before the start of the march for peace and responsibility, Baltimore prosecutors had announced the impending arrests of the six police officers who had detained, restrained, and transported Gray. Freddie Gray's death was ruled a homicide. A police report said that the circumstances of his arrest and transport were illegal, and had led to his death. The six officers were charged with crimes ranging from wrongful arrest to third-degree murder. All six had turned themselves in that day, and it seemed probable that they were now being processed at the city's main lockup on Greenmount Avenue.

The march was one of many that week. From Tuesday morning to Friday afternoon, there had been dozens of demonstrations. Most were peaceful. People would gather at the site of a burned-out building, or a previous altercation, and someone would arrive with a bullhorn, and begin calling out directives. Sometimes they just gave speeches until the crowd thinned. Other times the crowds would start moving, and a march would develop. There had been marches that barely covered a block, while others traveled for miles. Some crowds seemed to thin out as they traveled, while others attracted new marchers.

This one had begun with a rally outside City Hall. About a thousand people attended. As they started to move, a new objective developed: the City Jail. There was no certainty that the accused officers were there, but that wasn't the point. This was certainly no lynch mob, and a visit to the jail wasn't just about police—it was about the thousands of accused suspects and convicts who passed through there every year. Most were suspects accused of crimes and awaiting trial. On that typical day, there were about four thousand inmates. It was assumed that the six accused officers had joined their ranks.

As marchers closed in on the jail, the police told leaders they couldn't let the march stop there. The leaders hadn't made any formal decision to halt at the jail, and not wanting to risk any violence, they decided to just pass by, and head to the nearby train station. As the crowd walked by the jail's entrance, many talked to one another about people they knew inside. It seemed as if most of the protestors knew someone behind bars. In many Baltimore neighborhoods, jail time is a permanent part of the landscape as are drug addiction and joblessness.

On the surface, Freddie Gray's death raised issues of police brutality and racism. Six officers had manhandled a suspect, violating his rights, as well as standard police procedures. But as events played out in Baltimore, Gray's plight came to symbolize issues beyond that of police behavior. Soon the legitimacy of the nation's approach to crime and punishment came into question. The media began to notice the persistence of unemployment among African-Americans, even in the midst of economic recovery. Inevitably these concerns led to related issues, including the mass incarceration of Americans that's been a tenet of national policy for two generations.

As the marchers moved through Baltimore's streets, they were walking through neighborhoods whose male populations have declined due to unchallenged arrests, high-pressure plea bargains, and lengthy prison sentences. For many poor families, jail visits are as much a part of life as school, church, sports, or shopping. 620,000 people live in Baltimore. Four thousand people live in their jail system. This proportion holds for the whole nation. There are about 320 million Americans; 2.2 million of them go to bed each night behind bars. 840,000, or about 38%, are African-American, and 440,000, or about 20%, are Hispanic. About 90% are males. When African-American males get out, their job prospects are dismal. Nearly half won't find full-time work in their first year on the outside. That's a major factor in the 33% unemployment rate among males in Freddie Gray's West Baltimore neighborhood.

This wasn't always true. In 1970 less than two hundred thousand Americans were in prison. If that number had grown just enough to keep up with overall population growth, we would have just over three hundred thousand prisoners today. Instead, we have seven times that. Why? The following story is typical:

Jamal grew up on the streets of West Baltimore, where jobs are scarce, and young black men are almost expected to serve time in jail. His father did it twice, once for stealing cars, and again for drug dealing. When Jamal's dad heard he was wanted for the third time, he left the state, without telling anyone where he was headed. Jamal's older brother, Ahmad, was in jail too, serving six months in juvenile detention before he turned eighteen. Ahmad then got a thirty-day sentence in the city lockup for the destruction of property. Now that he was an adult, they put him in with the older convicts. That was enough. Ahmad looked in the mirror and saw himself turning into a string of bad statistics. He got out, got straight, and now he's studying to be a mortician.

Sometimes even Jamal's female relatives end up in jail. His mother did time for drug possession, and his aunt spent two months in lockup after assaulting an officer.

As a young boy, Jamal showed promise. During his first years in school, he discovered the pleasures of reading. He'd grown up in crowded apartments where TVs and radios were constantly blaring. Ahmad helped Jamal hook up to the Internet, but Jamal only used that for games and research for school assignments. What Jamal liked best was to find a private corner, put in earplugs to ward off the noise, and escape to other worlds through reading. He was literate, yet his schoolwork was often sloppy, late, or nonexistent. Whenever he put down the book he was reading, he got up and went back out to the streets of his neighborhood, with their drugs, crime, violence, and the constant threat of arrest and prison.

As Jamal grew from a small boy into a teenager, he began to attract attention from the local police. The officers who patrolled his neighborhood never caught Jamal red-handed, but he'd been spotted near enough incidents to make them feel he was guilty of something. During Jamal's teenaged years, the police stopped him every few weeks. Sometimes it seemed as if it were on their schedule. On three occasions, they took him into the station and held him until an adult came to take him home. One time they actually arrested him for disorderly conduct. He spent that night at Central Booking, before being released. The charge was dropped.

During those years, Jamal did participate in crimes. Three times, when his mother was going into withdrawal, he used his own money to buy her a fix. Once he snorted heroin himself, but it made him sick. Once a friend asked Jamal to keep a backpack for him. Jamal agreed, and after his friend left, Jamal looked inside. There he found a .44 magnum. Jamal was certain the gun had been stolen from a nearby drugstore in a break-in the weekend before, but he held the bag and its contents until his friend asked him to return them. It wouldn't have occurred to Jamal to do otherwise.

In high school, Jamal started getting serious. He studied hard and made sure all his courses were college-prep. When he had a hard time finding part-time work, he put in more hours on his studies. When he realized he had a problem with algebra, he got tutoring. As senior year came to a close, Jamal was accepted at the University of Maryland, and he qualified for enough financial aid to get him in the door. On the night of his senior prom, his future looked better than it ever had.

Though he didn't have a car, Jamal had gotten his license before most of his friends got theirs. When he'd asked his girlfriend, Alicia, to the prom, he'd promised that he'd pick her up in "something special." His older cousin had told Jamal that he knew of a car that would be available. "A brother owes me some favors, and he's got a classic red Mustang," said his cousin, "1964 convertible—man! What a car!" His cousin left the house the day before the prom and returned that evening with the Mustang. "It's yours for forty-eight hours," he said, "then I got to take it back to my buddy."

Jamal felt like a king, picking up Alicia in that Mustang. They arrived at the hall, parked near the entrance, and got out to the whistles and catcalls of their classmates. The prom was like a dream until a friend came in and pulled Jamal aside. "Did you lend your car to someone?" the friend asked. "No," said Jamal. "Then it's been stolen," the friend said.

Outside Jamal stared at the vacant parking space and started to sweat. "You should call the police," said his friend, but Jamal refused. He suddenly realized that he didn't even know the name of his cousin's "friend." He was trying to figure out what to do when Vice Principal Adams came out.

"I've been looking for you," the vice principal said. "I was out here almost a half hour ago when I saw two young men messing with the convertible top on that Mustang. It's yours, isn't it?"

Jamal said: "A friend of my cousin owns it."

"Oh . . . well . . . they'd gotten it started before I could get to them, but I did call the police. I'm surprised they're not here yet."

The police arrived a moment later. Jamal explained himself as well as he could, but they couldn't find his cousin. They told Jamal he would have to come to the station to officially report the theft. When he asked if he could do that the next day, they grew suspicious. An officer asked Jamal to get in the backseat of a police cruiser. Jamal complied.

While Jamal was at the station, the police found the Mustang in a nearby parking lot. One fender was dented, but it was otherwise intact. The car turned out to have already been reported as stolen nearly a month earlier. Police found quite a few prints, but the only matches turned out to be Jamal's. Jamal's cousin was still absent, and his prints weren't on file. No one knew the precise time or date the car had been stolen. It had been parked outside the owner's home in Bethesda, less than an hour away. Jamal couldn't prove he hadn't stolen it. The police felt they had enough evidence to convict him. They didn't look for his cousin, and they expressed total disbelief in the existence of his cousin's friend.

The court appointed a public defender to defend Jamal. This lawyer saw her job as damage control. She knew the system was stacked against her clients, so she accepted reality, and did her best to keep them from falling into worst-case scenarios. Like Jamal, all of them had a story proving their innocence. The lawyer spent most of her time persuading her clients to accept "reasonable" plea bargains. She was good at it.

Though Jamal insisted on his innocence, eight days in jail wore him down. Finally, his lawyer told him she could probably get him off on the car theft if he would plead guilty to the lesser charge of possession of the stolen property.

"You did have possession of it," she reminded him.

"But I had no idea that it was stolen."

"We can go to trial on the car theft charge, but if you lose, three years is a certainty. Often they ask five. If we cop a plea, I can get you off with a year, maybe less. On a similar case last year I got the judge to agree to time served. I can't promise anything like that, but you never know."

"But once I'm convicted, what chance have I got?" Jamal cried. "I thought about becoming a lawyer, but with a conviction on my record, I probably can't even get a student loan."

"If we can get the charge reduced, eventually we might get the record expunged," said his lawyer. "In the meantime, when you're applying for work, just don't say anything unless you're asked. Often these things just fade away."

Jamal finally agreed, but things didn't go as planned. The judge didn't like the deal, and when Jamal entered his plea, he got three years.

In Baltimore, there are thousands of Jamals, and in America, there are millions more. Each is a potential Freddie Gray. These young men of color grow up in a system that abandons them to a life of crime. Even if they resist it, that life can ensnare them. To these young men and their families, police are not protectors, courts are not places of justice, nor are they venues for learning the truth.

U.S. prisons are jammed with inmates like Jamal. Some of his fellow inmates are guilty of horrible crimes, but a huge number of them are like Jamal— young men who trusted the wrong person, then got caught up in law enforcement's net. 2.2 million prisoners, 840,000 men of color, nearly half of young black males unemployed—these numbers show us that something is wrong, but they don't reveal the stories. There are no statistics on young men like Jamal. There are only all those jail cells, each one with a prisoner.

If there had been good, affordable schools, most of these men would have gone to them. If there had been jobs, most of these men would have worked and avoided the snares of the system. If there had been a system that supported families, and neighborhoods with real community spirit, Jamal would have gone to law school instead of prison. But the only law Jamal knows is the one that put him in his cell. We must reinterpret that law, or write a new one so Jamal and his brothers can come out to a world that welcomes anyone who's willing to work for a better future.

About the Author

Malcolm Allen is a recognized expert on human potential and (BCSA) Board Certified Social Advocate. He migrates effortlessly between corporate boardrooms and underserved communities aiming to advance the interests of social justice, particularly on behalf of populations or groups who have been disadvantaged, disempowered, or forgotten.

Allen has authored over two dozen books, and most have achieved best-selling status. He has worked with subject matter experts and credentialed instruction designers to socially engineer a platform of outcome-based programs that provide solutions for disabled veterans, recidivism, human trafficking, dropout prevention, bullying, diversity, mentoring, financial inclusion, entrepreneurship, and leadership.

All programs are Military Approved, and available at Penn Foster College and Graduate America Centers of Excellence around the world. For seminar licensing, book purchases, or speaker requests, please visit: Unconditional.org